4 Practice Tests for the NNAT®2 (Naglieri Nonverbal Ability Test®)

Level D (Grades 3 & 4)

By Smart Cookie Ink

Printed in the United States of America.

INTRODUCTION

The Naglieri Nonverbal Ability Test® (NNAT®2) is a measure of general non-verbal analytical ability. This test is administered to K–12 school children as a means to identify potentially gifted children for placement in accelerated learning programs. The test utilizes a complex series of geometric shapes and designs in a progressive matrix to assess a child's critical thinking and analytical reasoning abilities.

A good score on the NNAT®2 qualifies a child for superior educational programs within public and private schools.

Critical thinking and analytical reasoning are seldom part of the standard school curriculum. Most children appear for the NNAT®2 without a clear understanding of what is expected of them. Sometimes even the brightest of young minds can be rattled because of unfamiliarity with the questions and test format. The shapes, diagrams and pictures in the test can be alien concepts forcing them to reflexively respond in the absence of a test taking strategy.

Schools suggest a good night's sleep and a healthy breakfast as adequate preparation – as well-intended as this advice may be, it just won't cut it in this increasingly competitive environment.

Help your child perform at his/her best AND ensure that his/her true potential is fairly and accurately evaluated!

With this in mind, we have designed this book with a specific purpose: to hone your child's critical thinking and analytical reasoning abilities that the NNAT® test demands.

The four NNAT®2 practice tests that this book offers will

- **Help tune your child's mind to think critically**

- **Provide varied exercises in all the areas of reasoning that the test considers:**
    - **Pattern Completion**
    - **Reasoning by Analogy**
    - **Serial Reasoning**
    - **Spatial Visualization**

- **Familiarize your child with the format of the test.**

In addition, the book also offers,

- **Important test taking tips and strategies**

Now, get ready to ace this test!

TABLE OF CONTENTS

TIPS FOR THE TESTERS

• A GOOD NIGHT'S SLEEP & A HEALTHY BREAKFAST!

The test is spread over 2 to 5 days in most school districts. Make sure you get a good night's sleep and eat a healthy breakfast and arrive to school on time on these important days of testing. A calm mind is usually able to think significantly better!

• I said "LISTEN!"

Listen to the instructions given to you during the examination. You will be given instructions on how to fill the test forms. Be sure to follow these instructions. You do not want to compromise your test score because you filled in the answers incorrectly or in the wrong section!

As you already may know, the NNAT® test is divided into multiple sections. You will be provided with directions at the start of each section. The directions will explain the section and tell you how the questions in it should be answered. Pay attention even though you may be familiar with the test format.

• WHAT IS IN YOUR MIND'S EYE?

Before looking at the answers, it might help if you try to first solve the question in your mind. This approach works well for some sections over others. Try it and judge for yourself.

• EVALUATE ALL ANSWER CHOICES!

Evaluate all answer choices and always choose the one right answer which BEST answers the question. Remember, sometimes the best available answer might not be the answer in your mind's eye. You are just choosing the best of the lot!

• SLASH THE TRASH!

If you can eliminate one or two obviously wrong answer choices at the first glance, you can focus on picking the correct answer from among the remaining choices.

• TAKE A GUESS!

NNAT® test scores are calculated based on the number of right answers. It is best to answer all questions rather than leave them blank. If after 'slashing the trash', you do not know the correct answer, guess from the available 'maybe' answers.

• COLOR THE BUBBLE!

It is important to know how to color the bubble. Sometimes, you may be given a bubble test form. At other times, you may have to color the bubbles just below the answer choices within the question paper. Practice coloring bubbles and using a sample bubble test form. Also remember to color only one bubble per question.

Practice Test 1
for the NNAT®2

Naglieri Nonverbal Ability Test®

Level D (Grades 3 & 4)

PATTERN COMPLETION

Each question in this section has a large rectangle with a picture or design. Within the large rectangle, there is a smaller rectangle with a question mark covering a section of the big rectangle. Pick the hidden part of the big rectangle and color the bubble under your choice.

1.

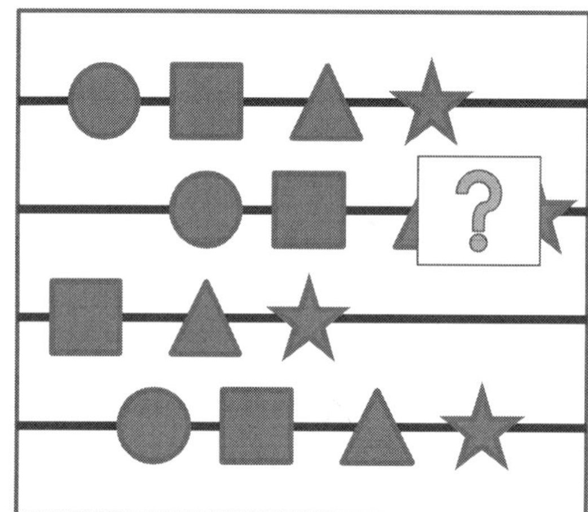

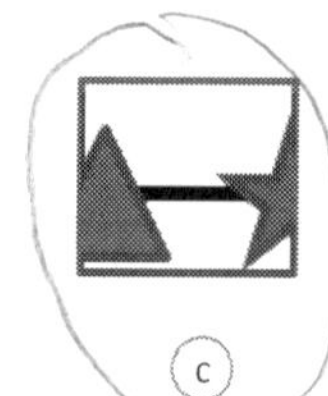

a b c d e

2.

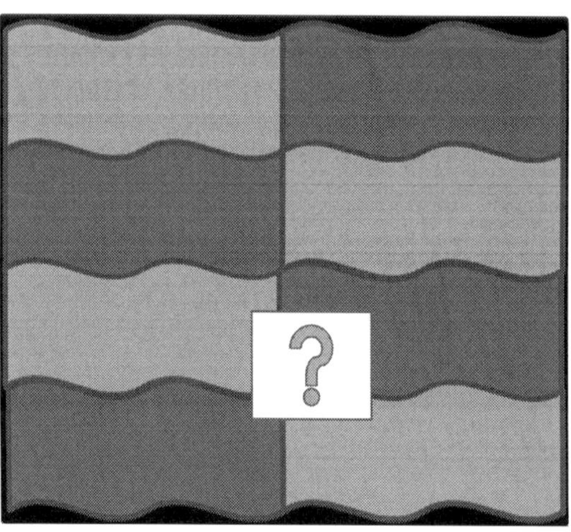

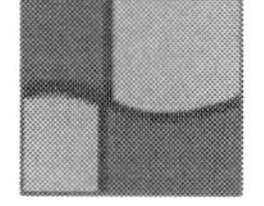

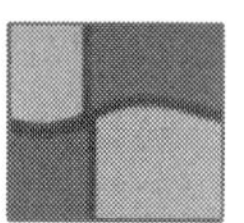

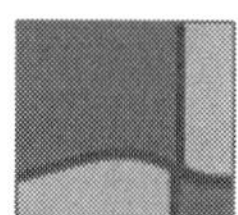

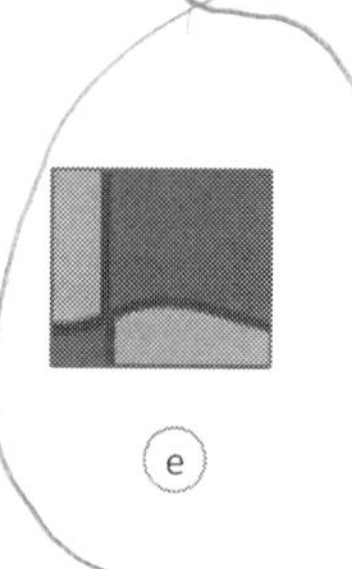

a b c d e

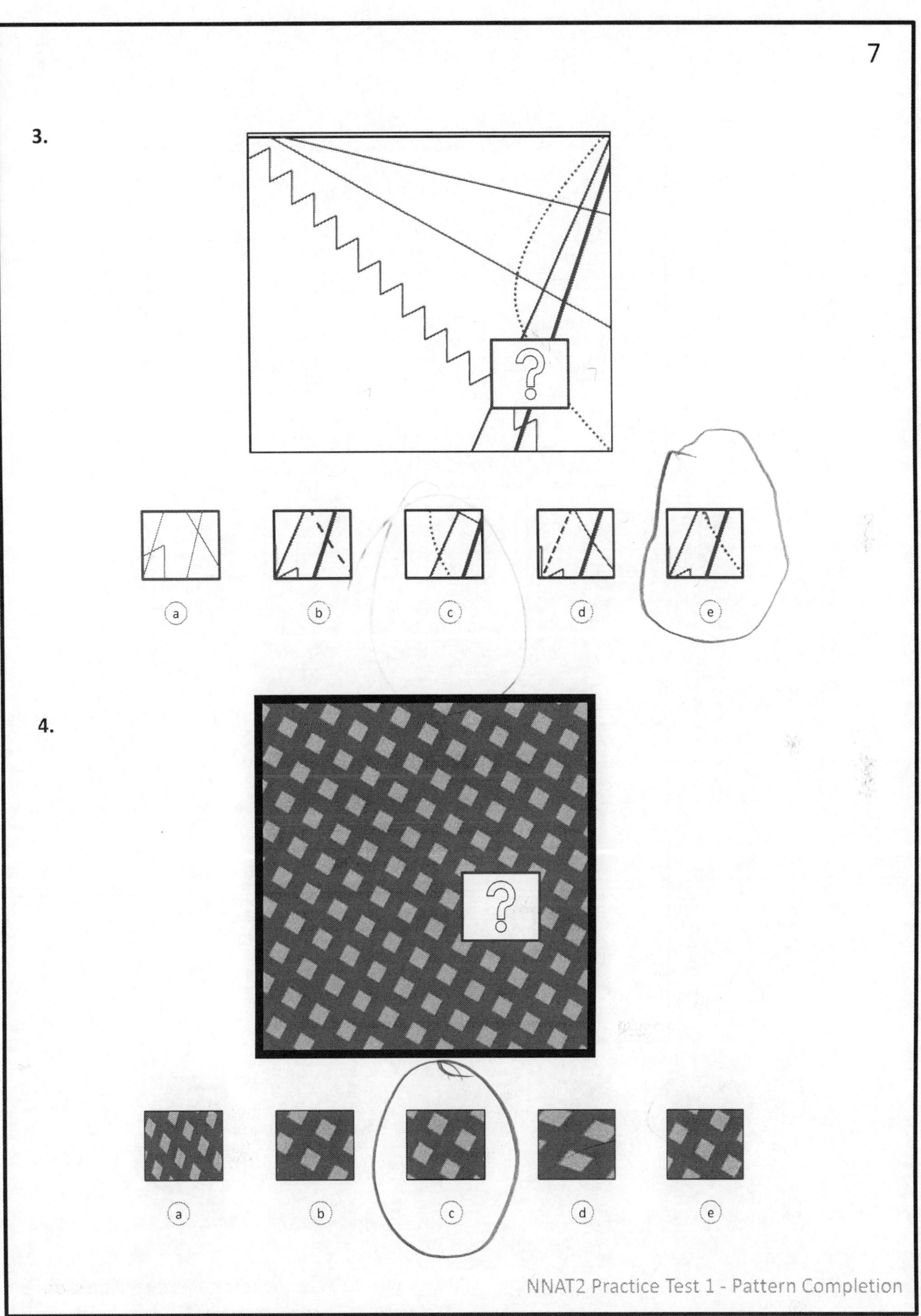
3.
a
b
c
d
e
4.
a
b
c
d
e

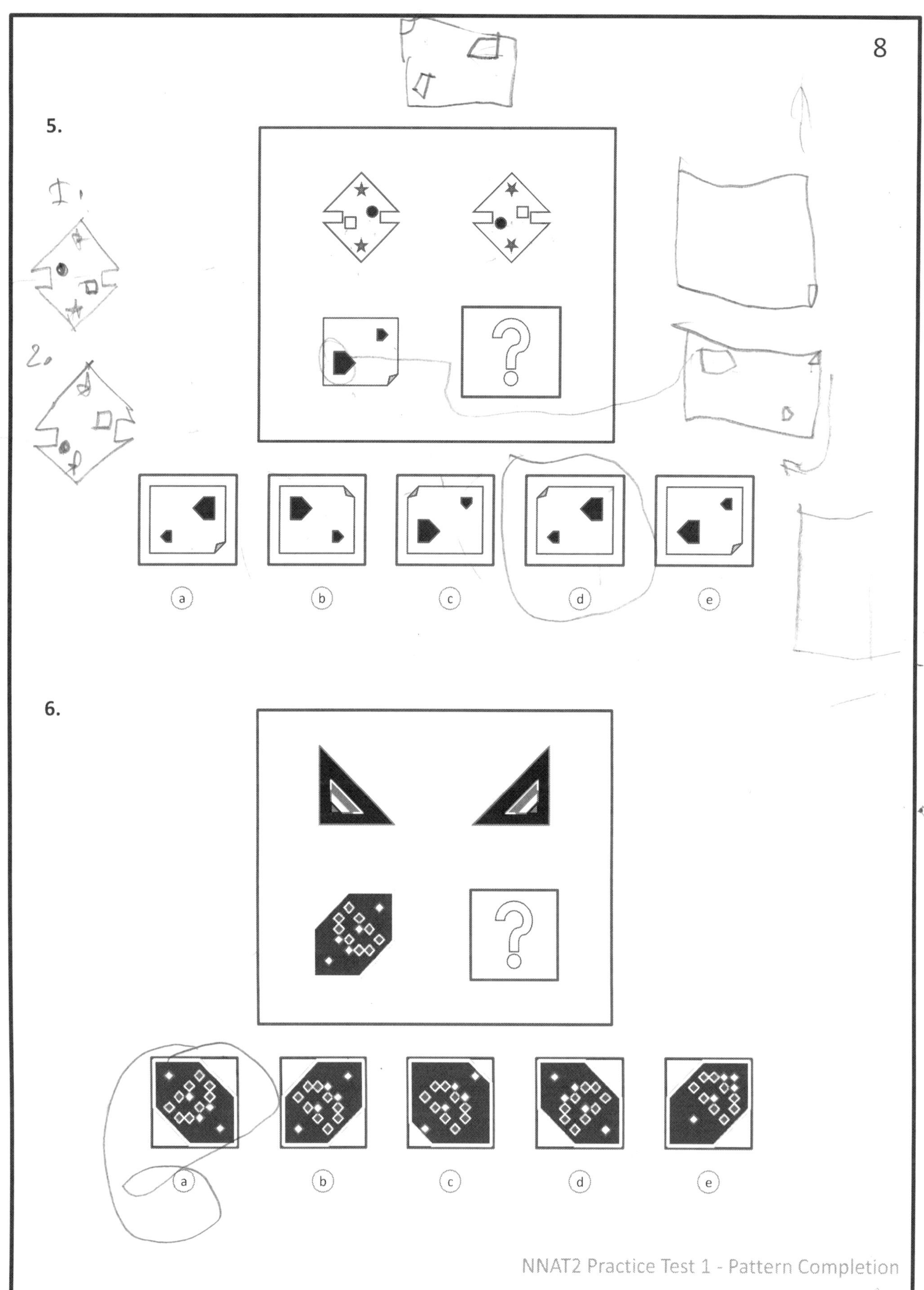

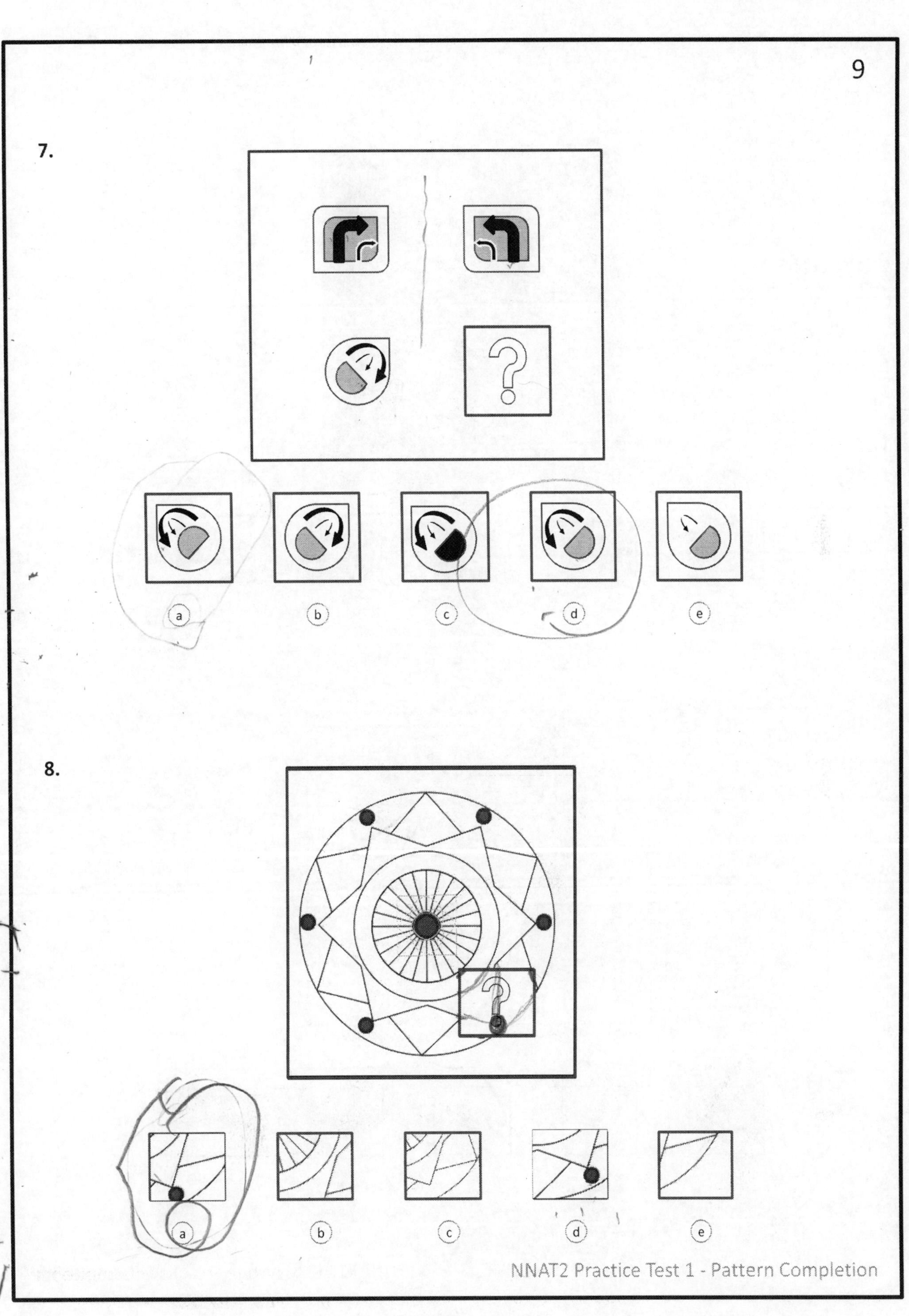
7.
a
b
c
d
e
8.
a
b
c
d
e

9.

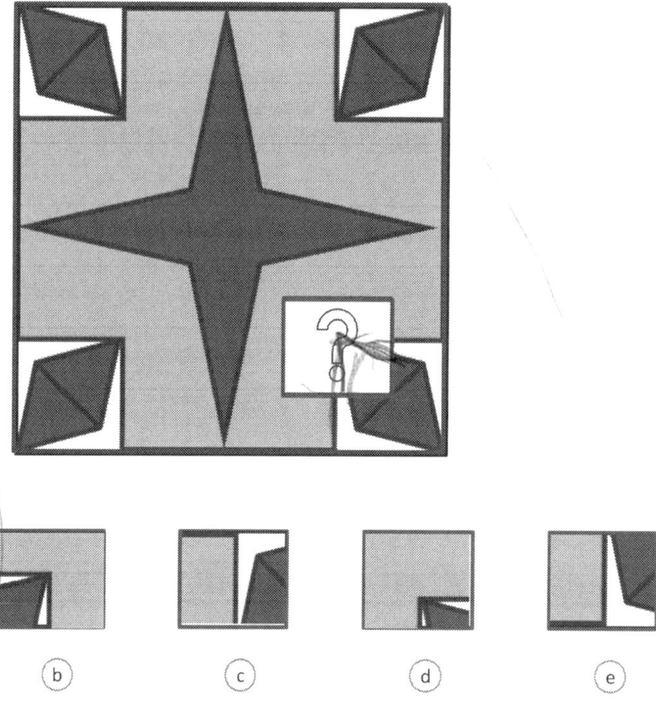

a b c d e

10.

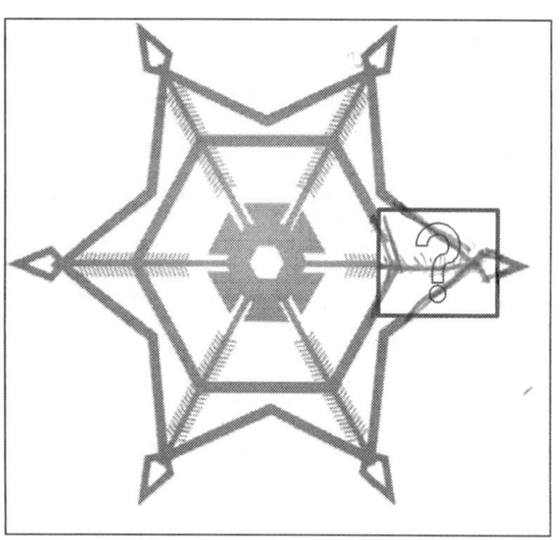

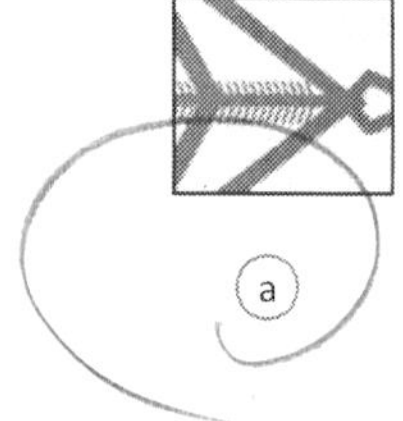

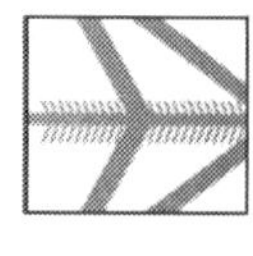
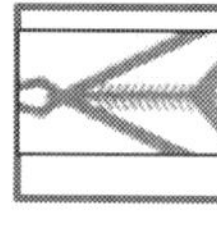

a b c d

REASONING BY ANALOGY

Each question in this section has three rows of pictures. In each row, determine how the picture changes as you go across the row. The same changes should be echoed across all the three rows. Pick the missing picture and color the bubble under your choice.

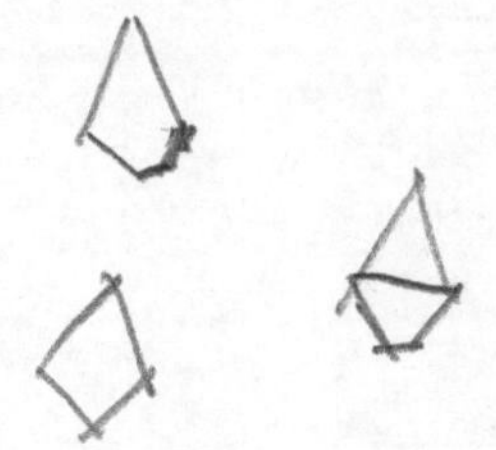

1.

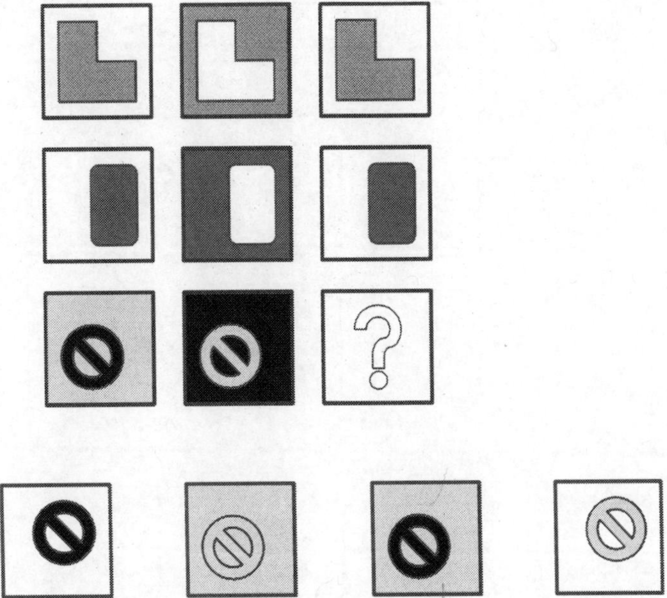

2.

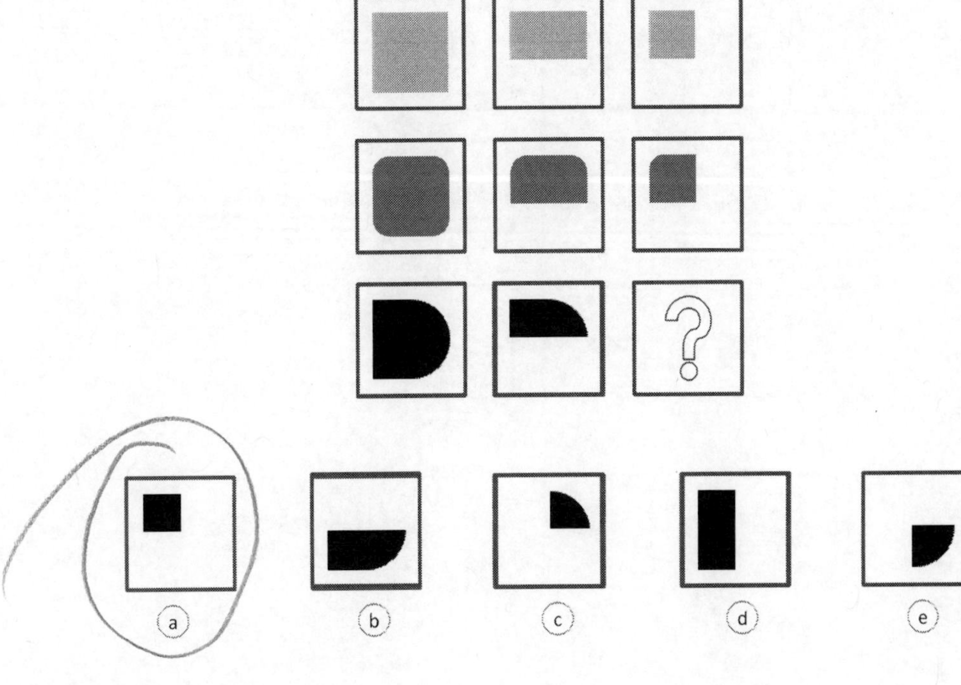

3.

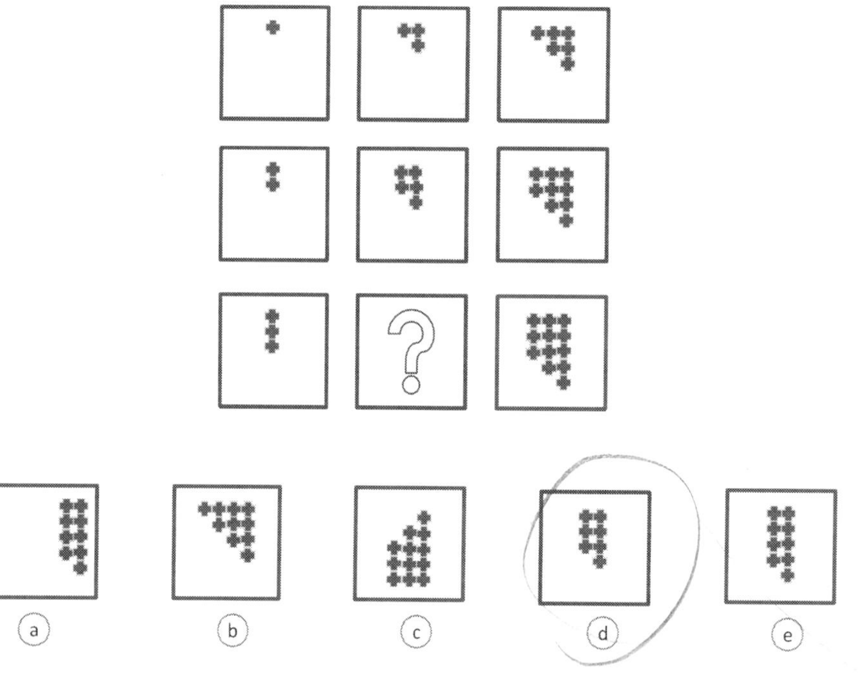

4.

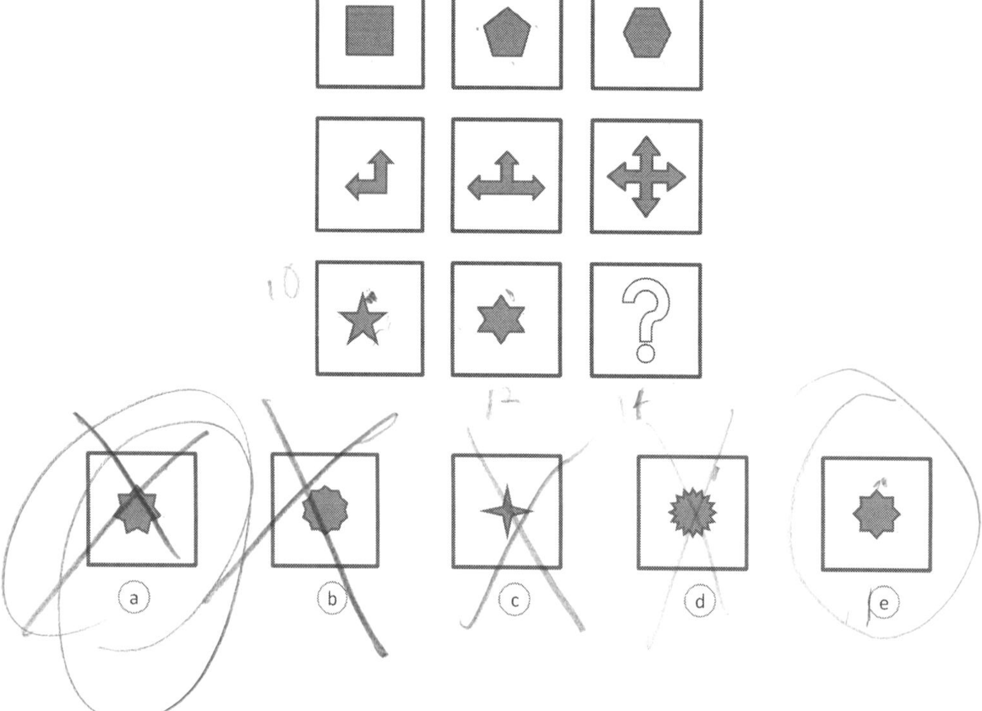

5.

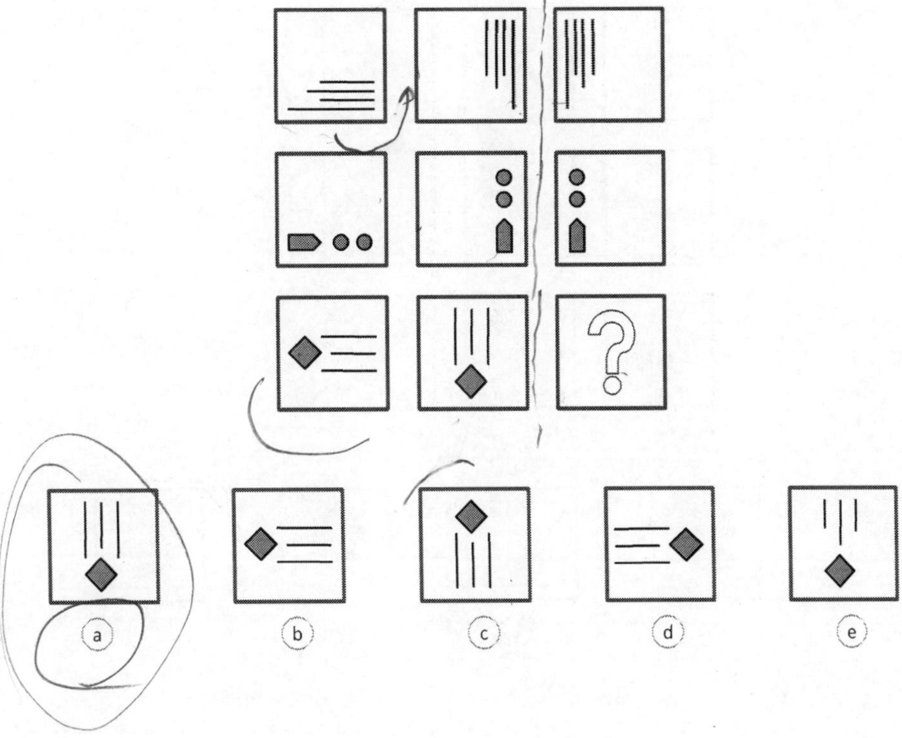

6.

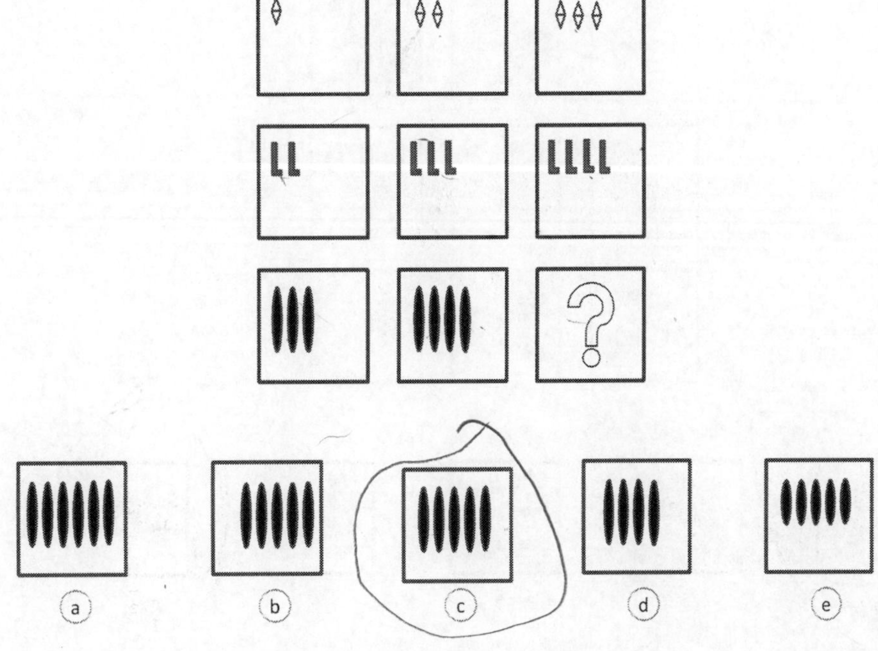

7.

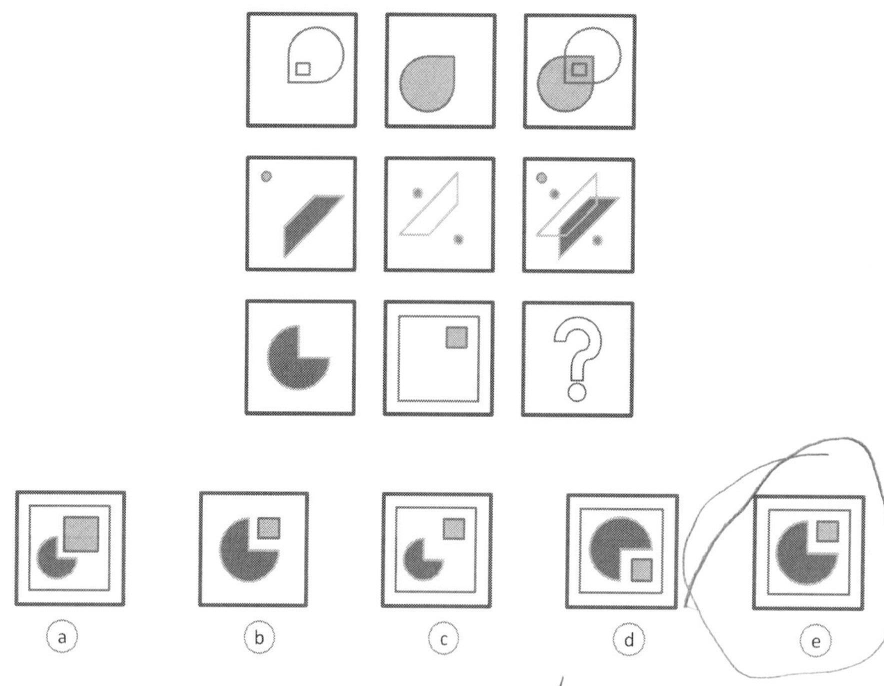

8.

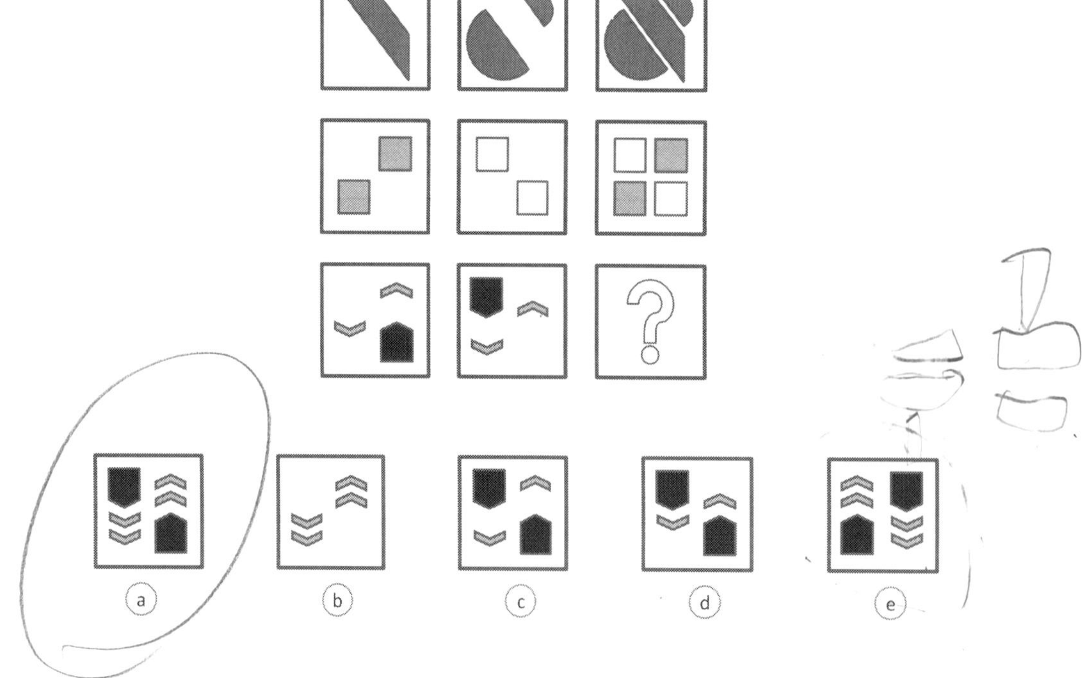

9.

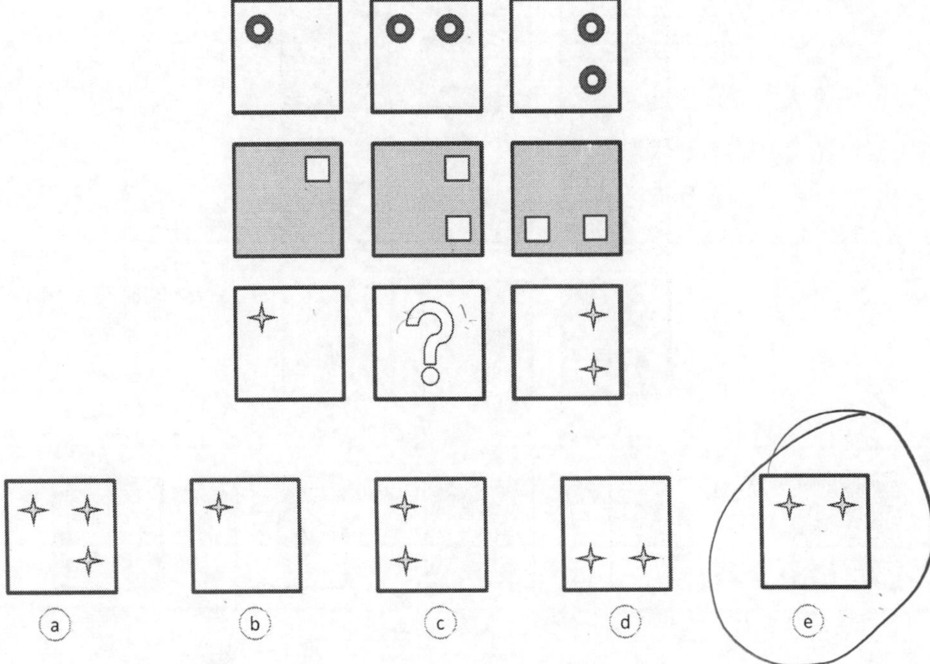

10.

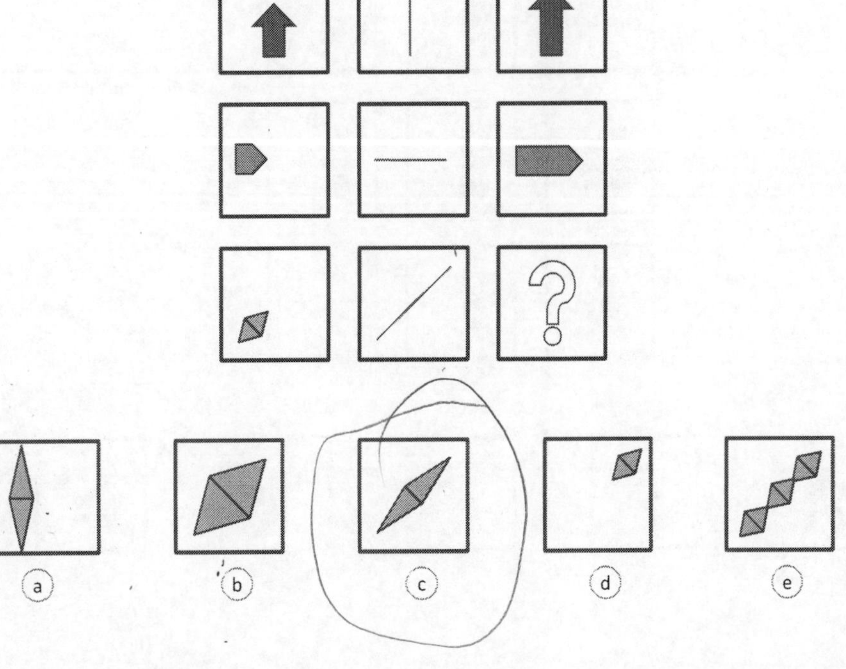

11.

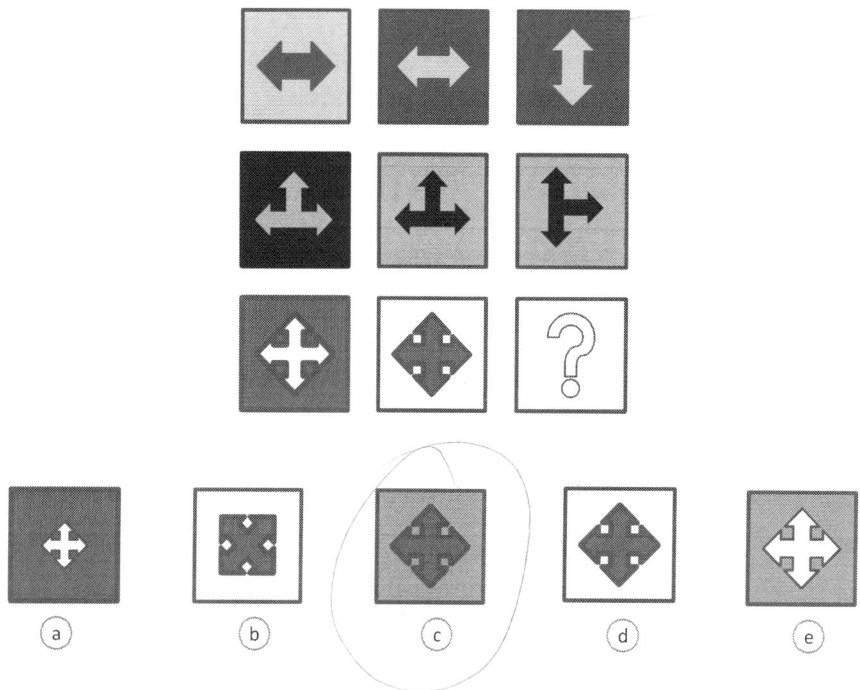

12.

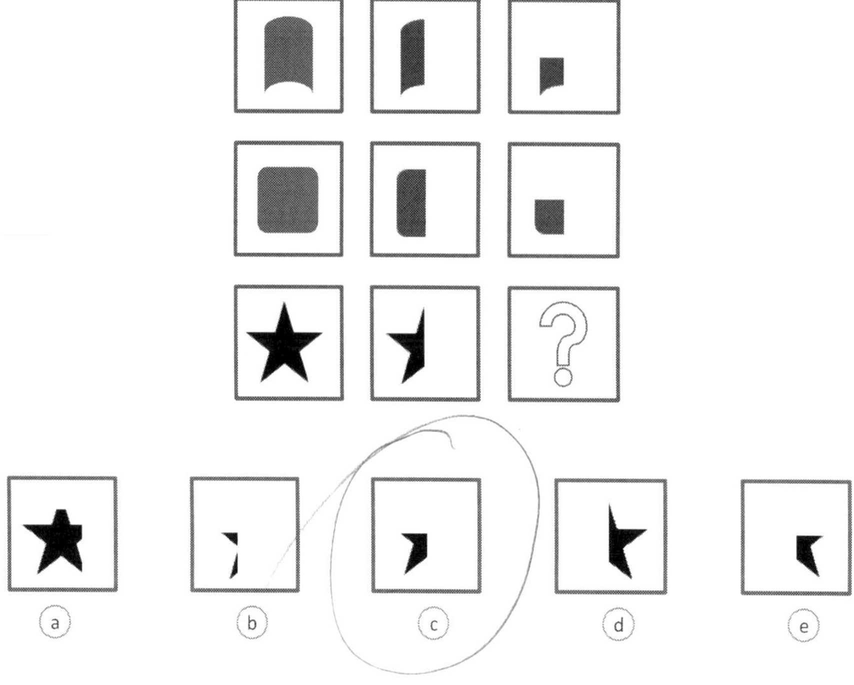

13.

14.

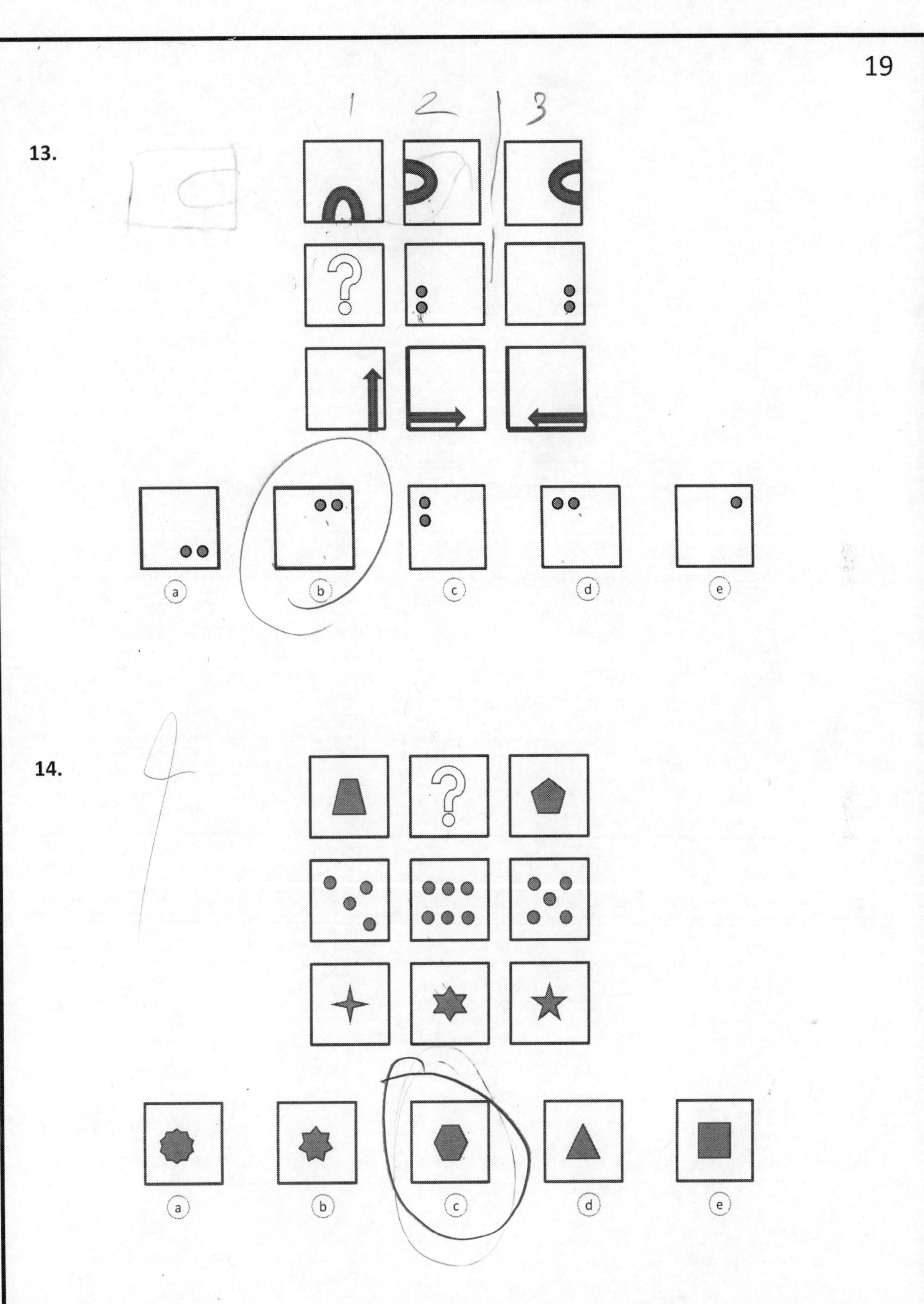

SERIAL REASONING

Each question in this section has a matrix of three rows and three columns. The pictures change as you go across the row and down the column in the matrix. Determine the change pattern within the matrix and pick the correct missing picture that will complete the matrix. Color the bubble under your choice.

1.

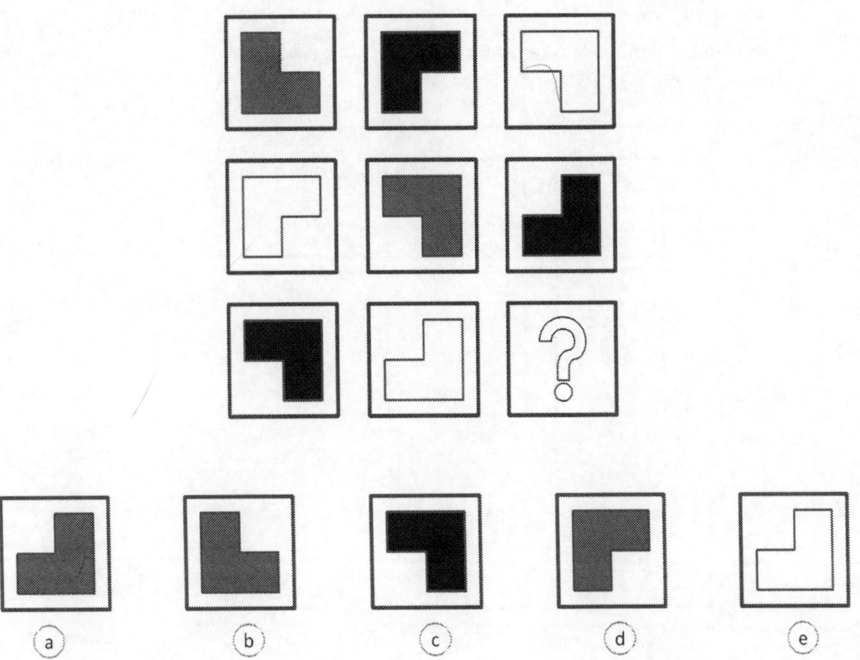

2.

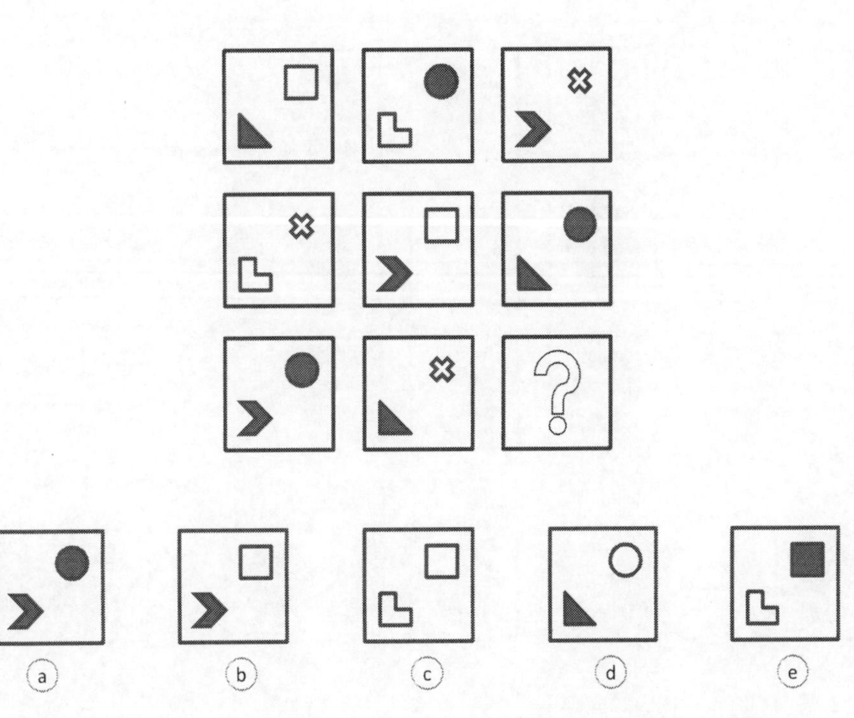

3.

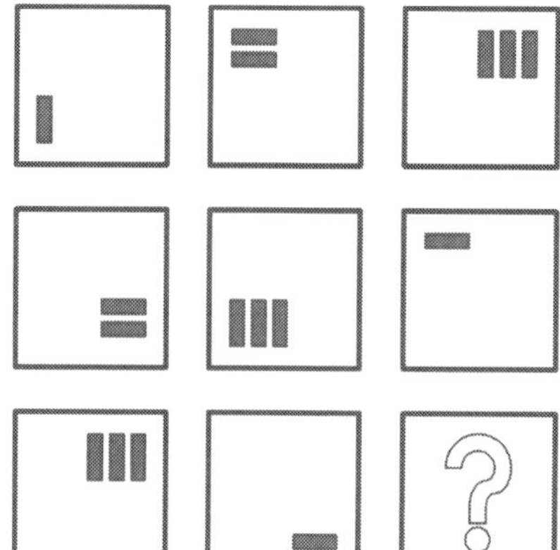

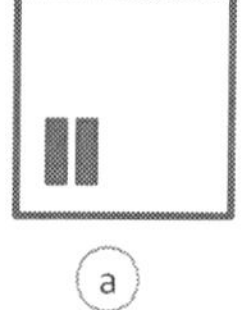
a

b

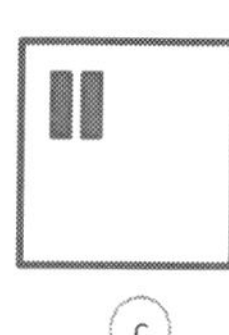
c

d

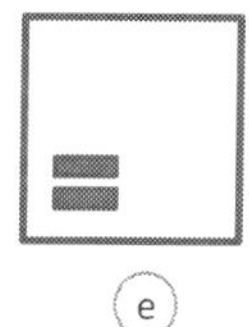
e

4.

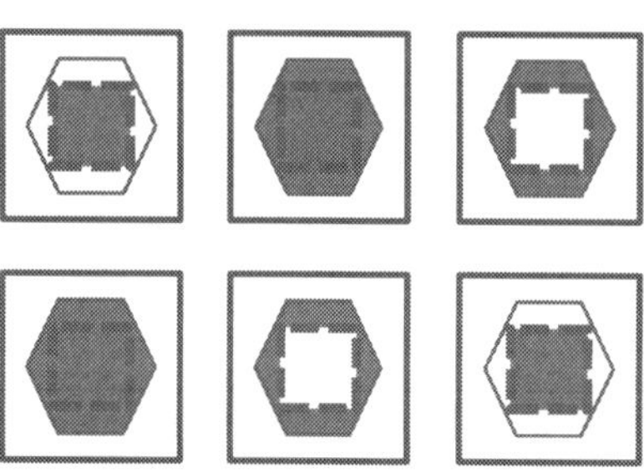

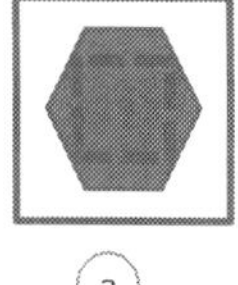
a

b

c

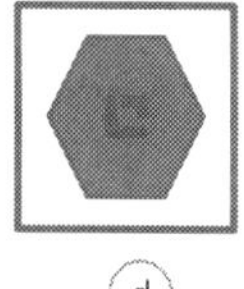
d

e

5.

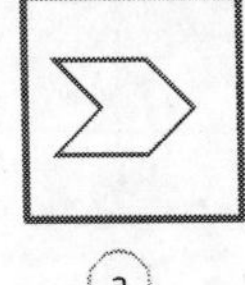
a

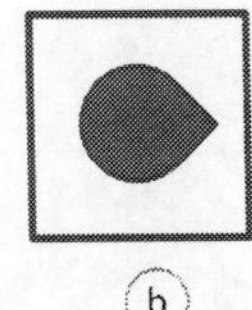
b

c

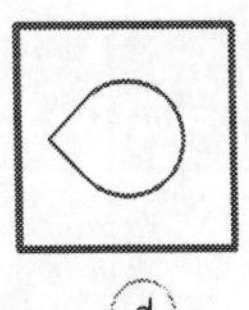
d

e

6.

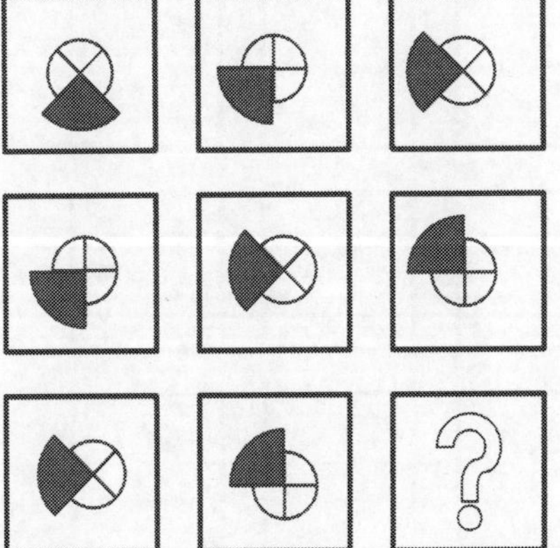

a

b

c

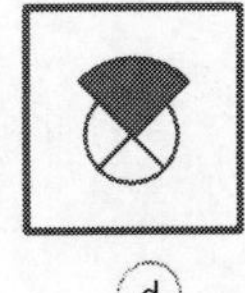
d

e

7.

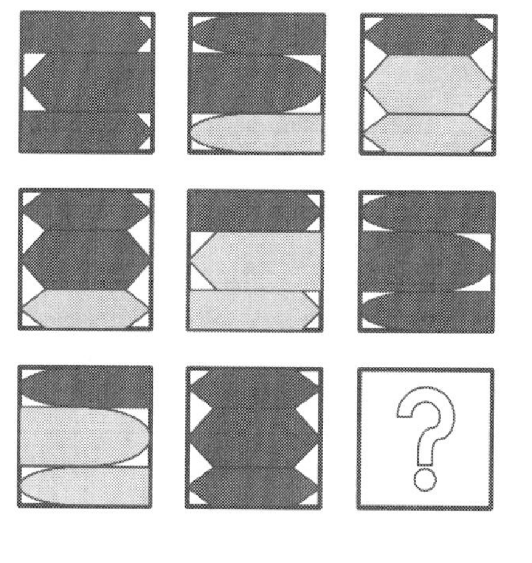

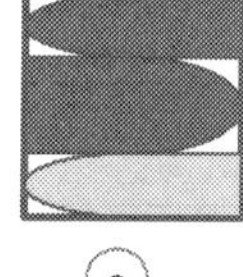
a

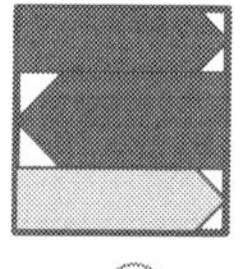
b

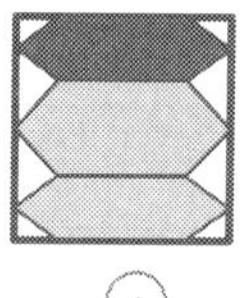
c

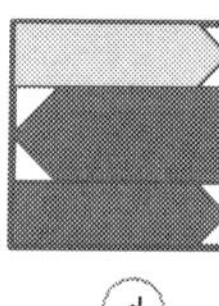
d

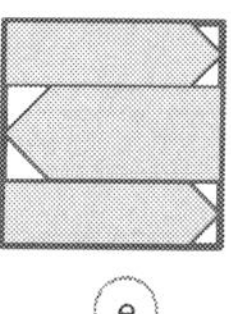
e

8.

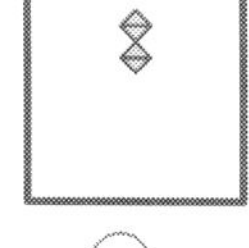
a

b

c

d

e

9.

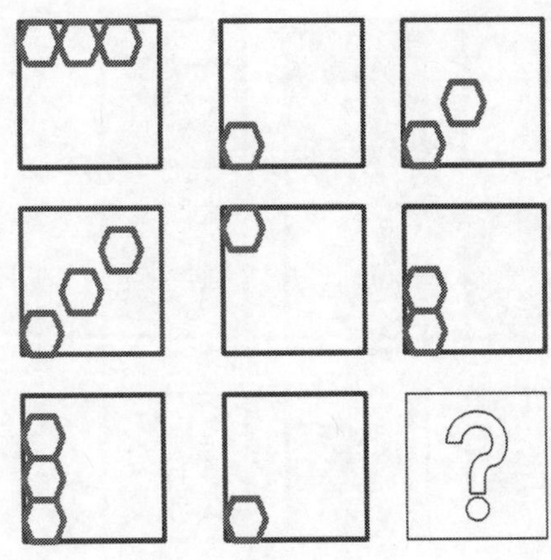

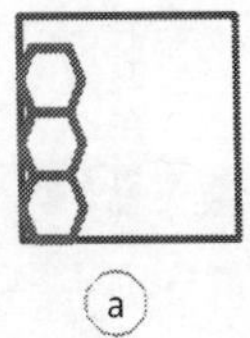
a

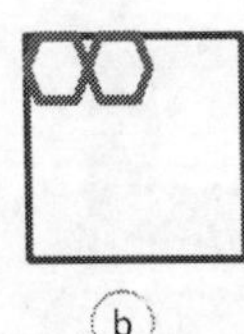
b

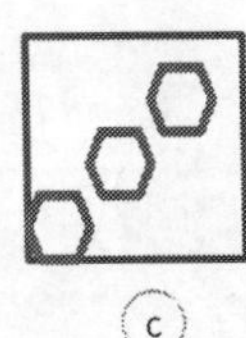
c

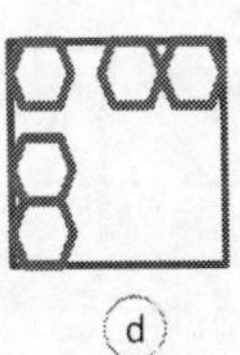
d

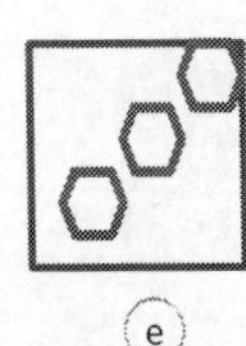
e

10.

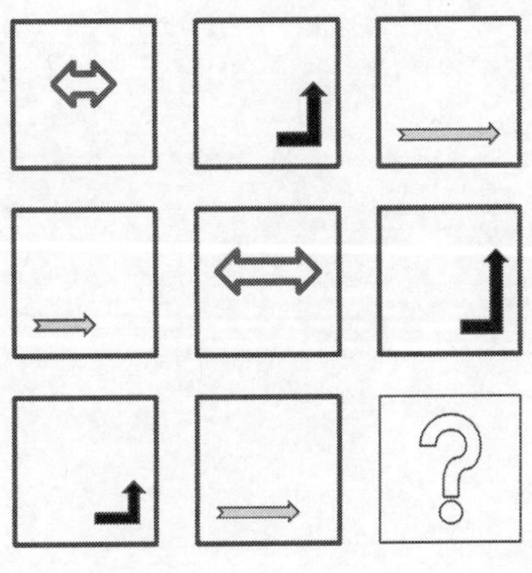

a

b

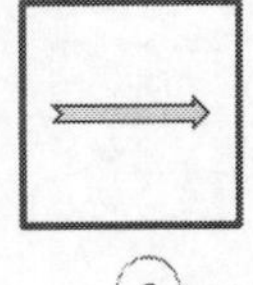
c

d

e

11.

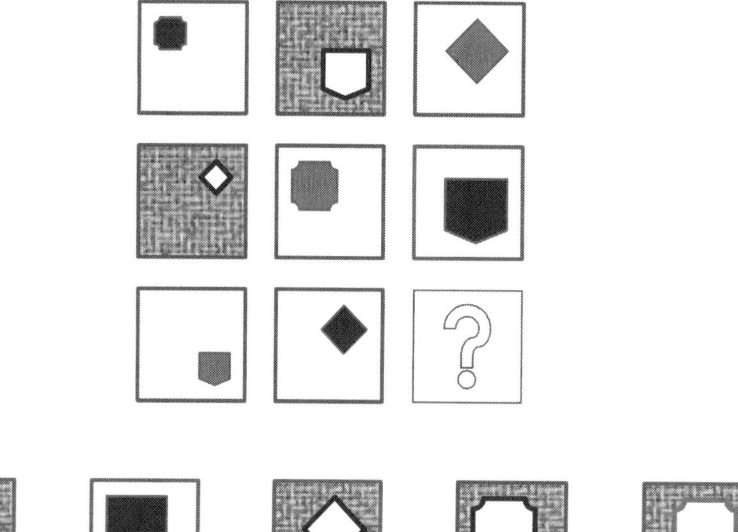

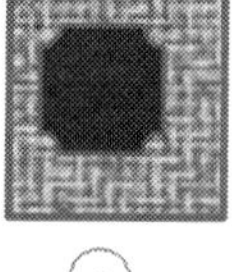
a

b

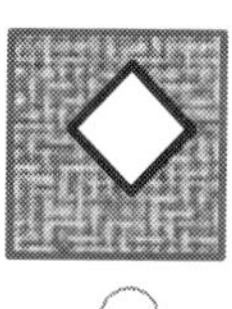
c

d

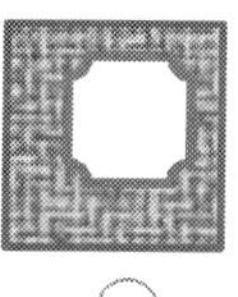
e

SPATIAL VISUALIZATION – SECTION A

Each question in this section has three pictures on the top row. The third picture in the row is formed by combining the first two pictures. Using the same principle, pick the missing picture in the bottom row. Color the bubble under your choice.

1.

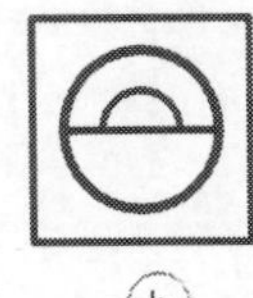

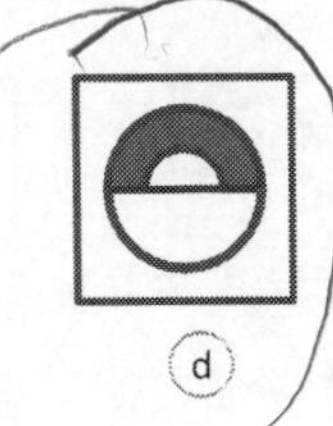

a b c d e

2.

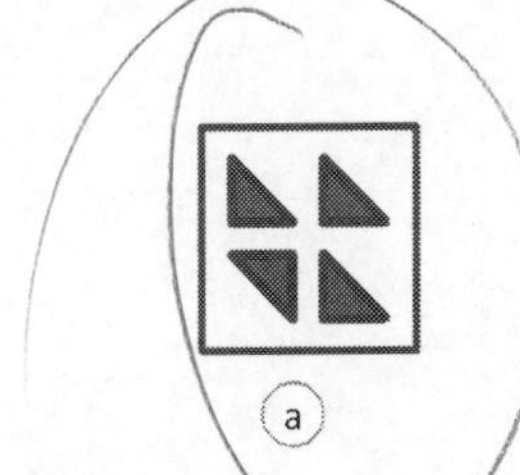

a b c d e

3.

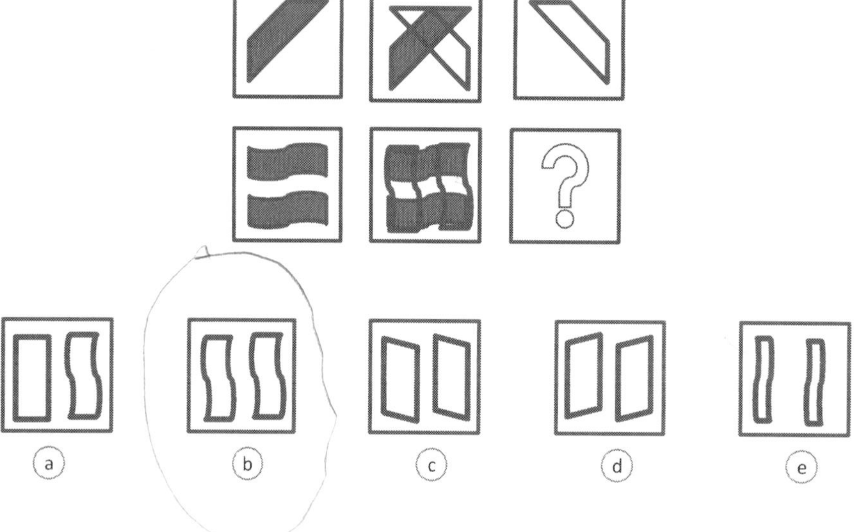

4.

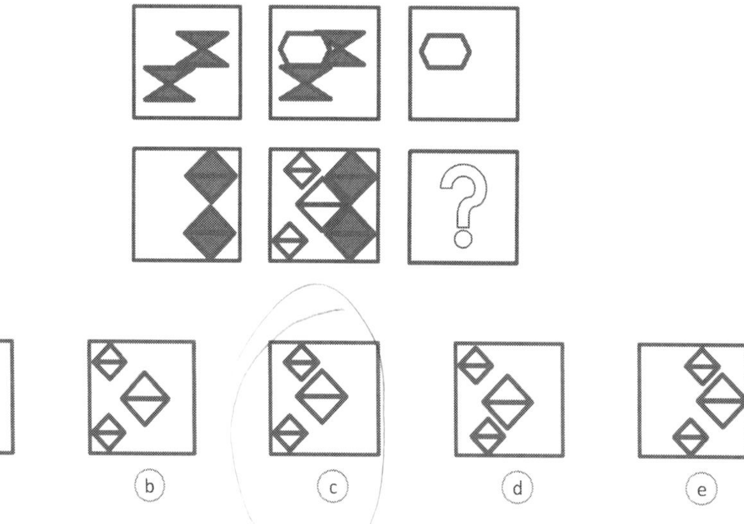

5.

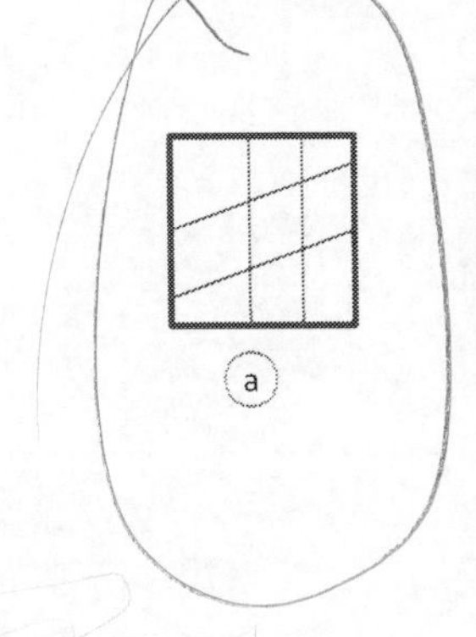

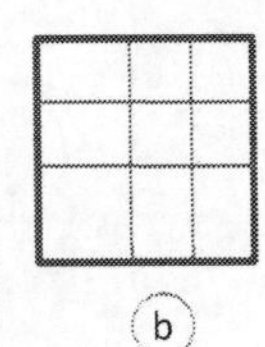

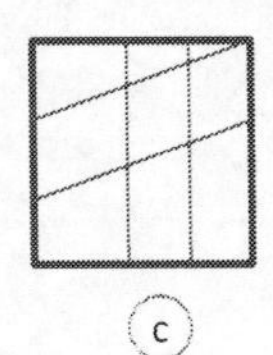

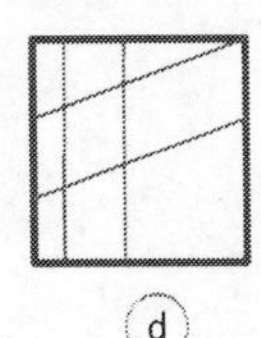

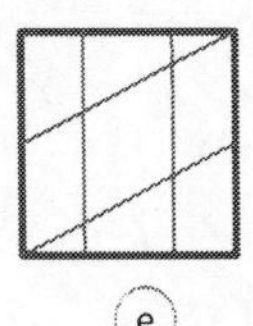

(a) (b) (c) (d) (e)

6.

(a) (b) (c) (d) (e)

SPATIAL VISUALIZATION – SECTION B

Each question in this section has two pictures on the top row. The picture on the right in the top row is created by folding the outside shapes into the main shape of the picture on the left. Now, pick the picture that would be created when the outside shapes in the second row are folded in the same manner as the first row. Color the bubble under your choice.

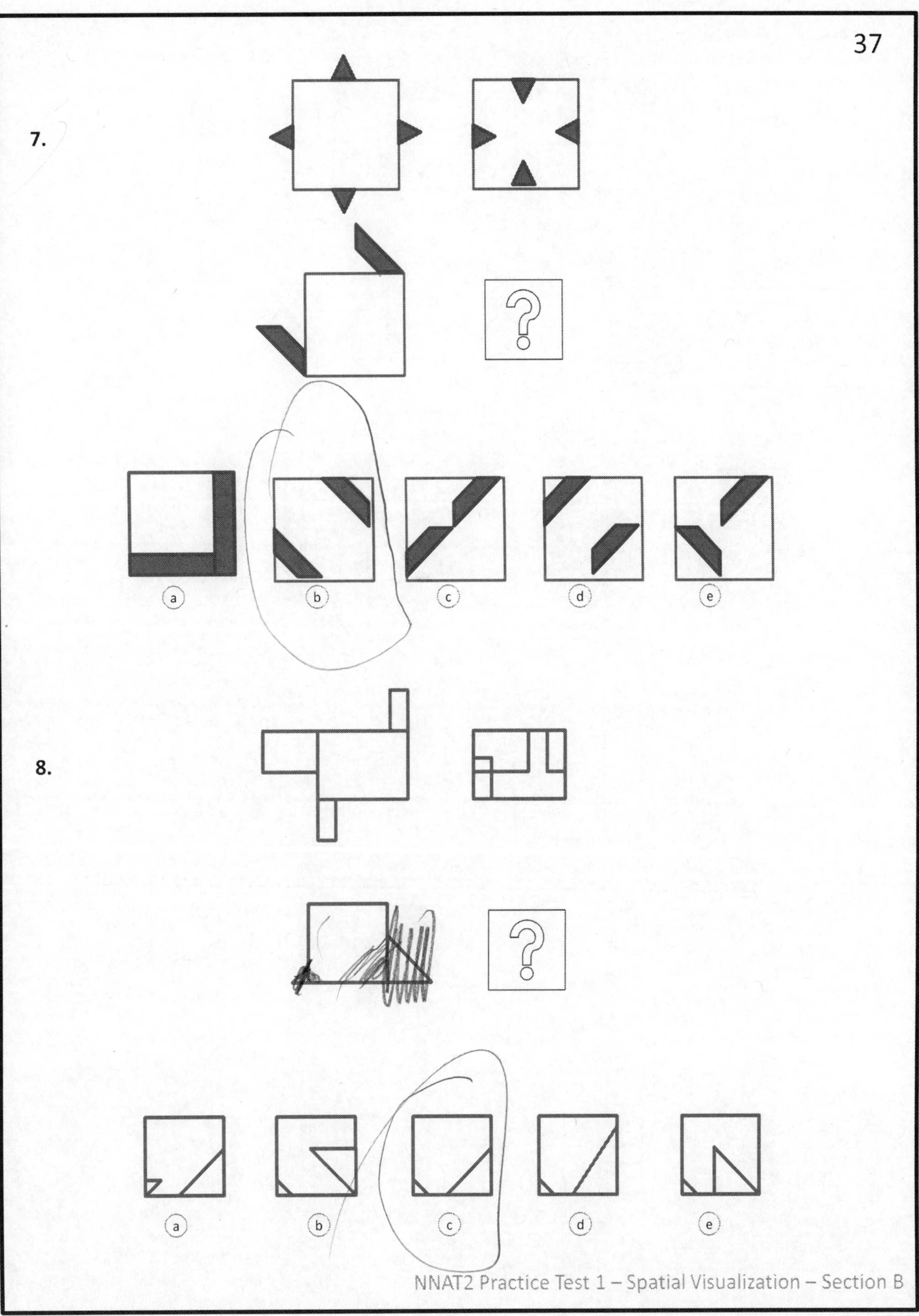
7.
a
b
c
d
e
8.
a
b
c
d
e

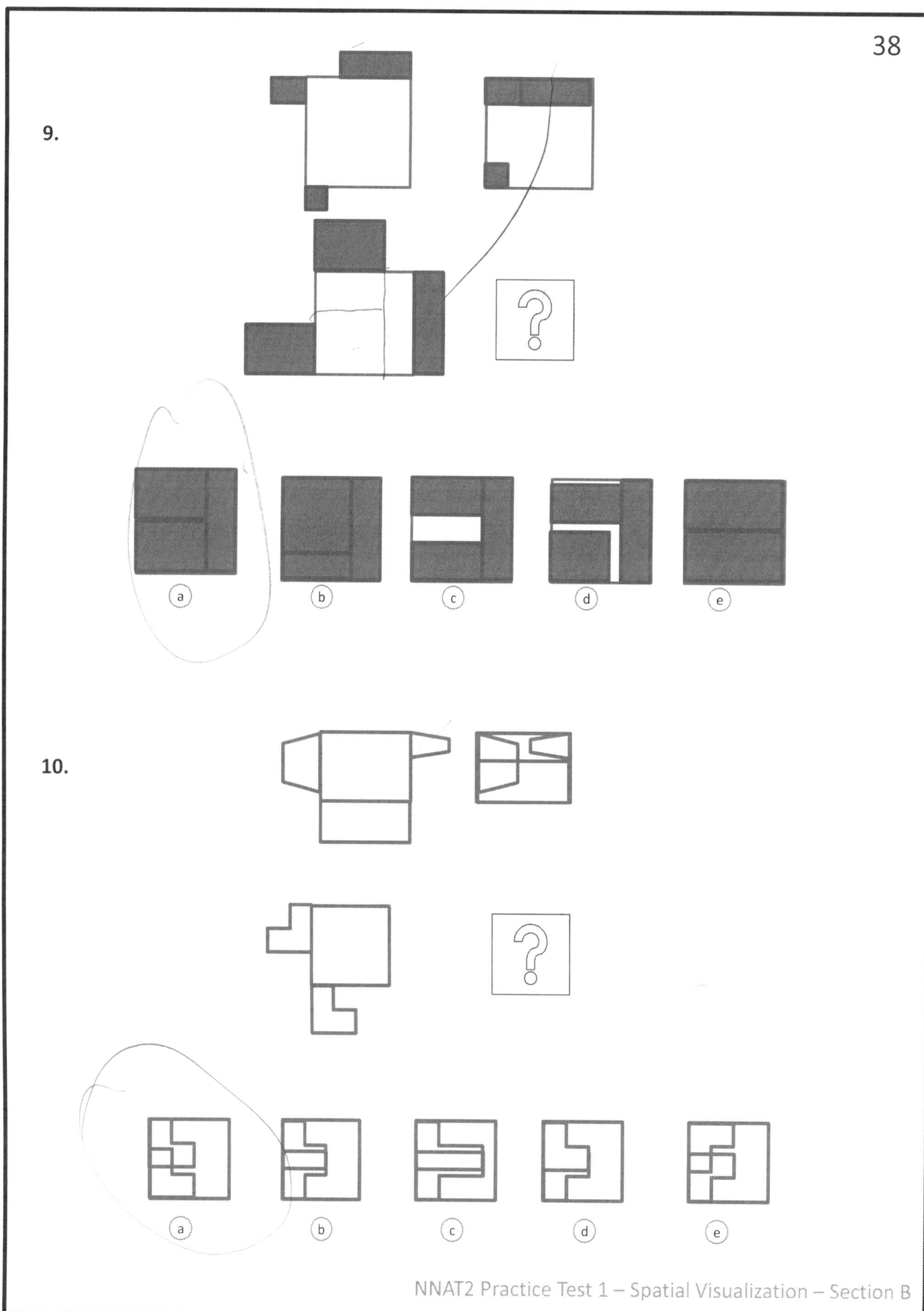
9.
a
b
c
d
e
10.
a
b
c
d
e

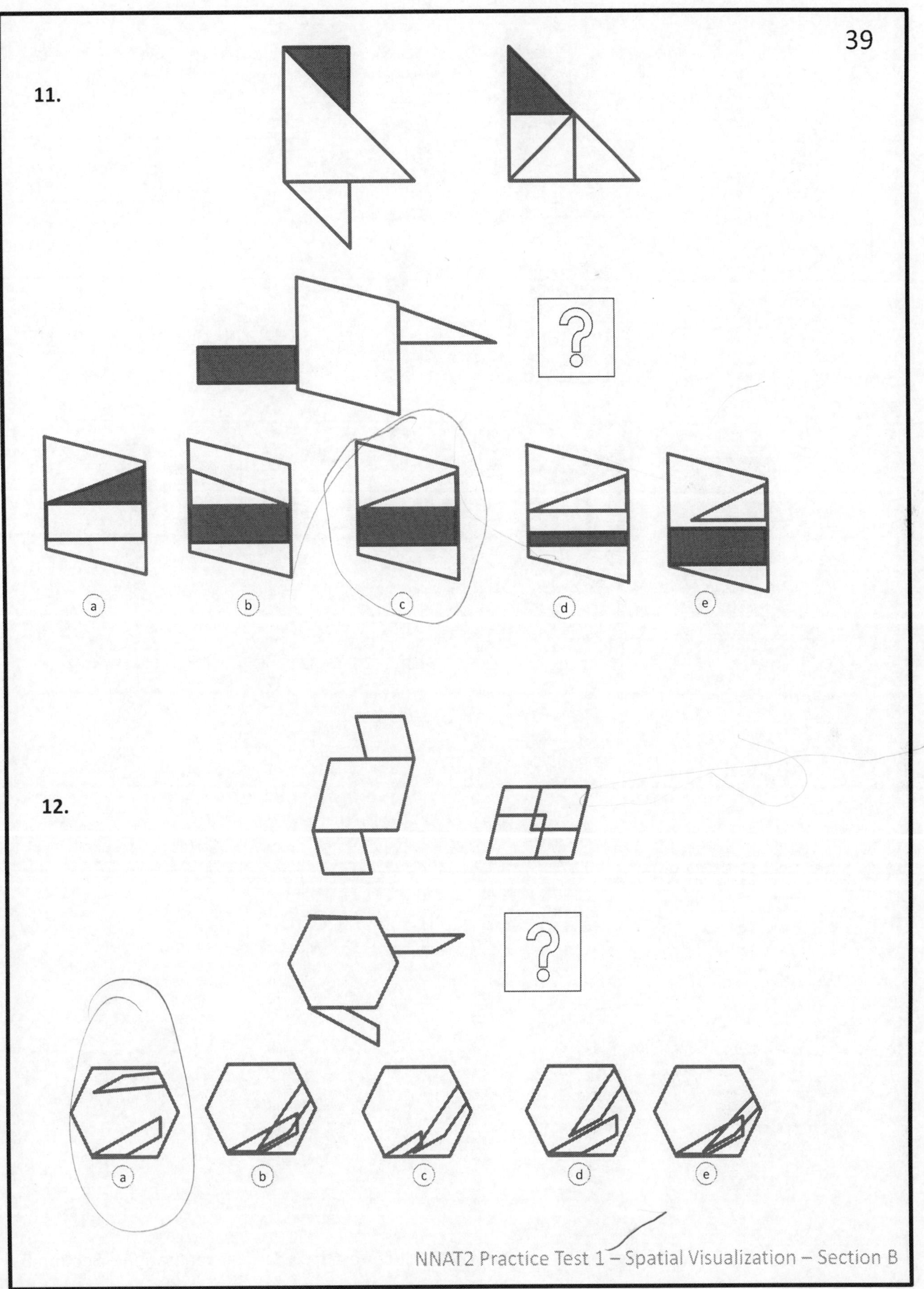
11.
a
b
c
d
e
12.
a
b
c
d
e

13.

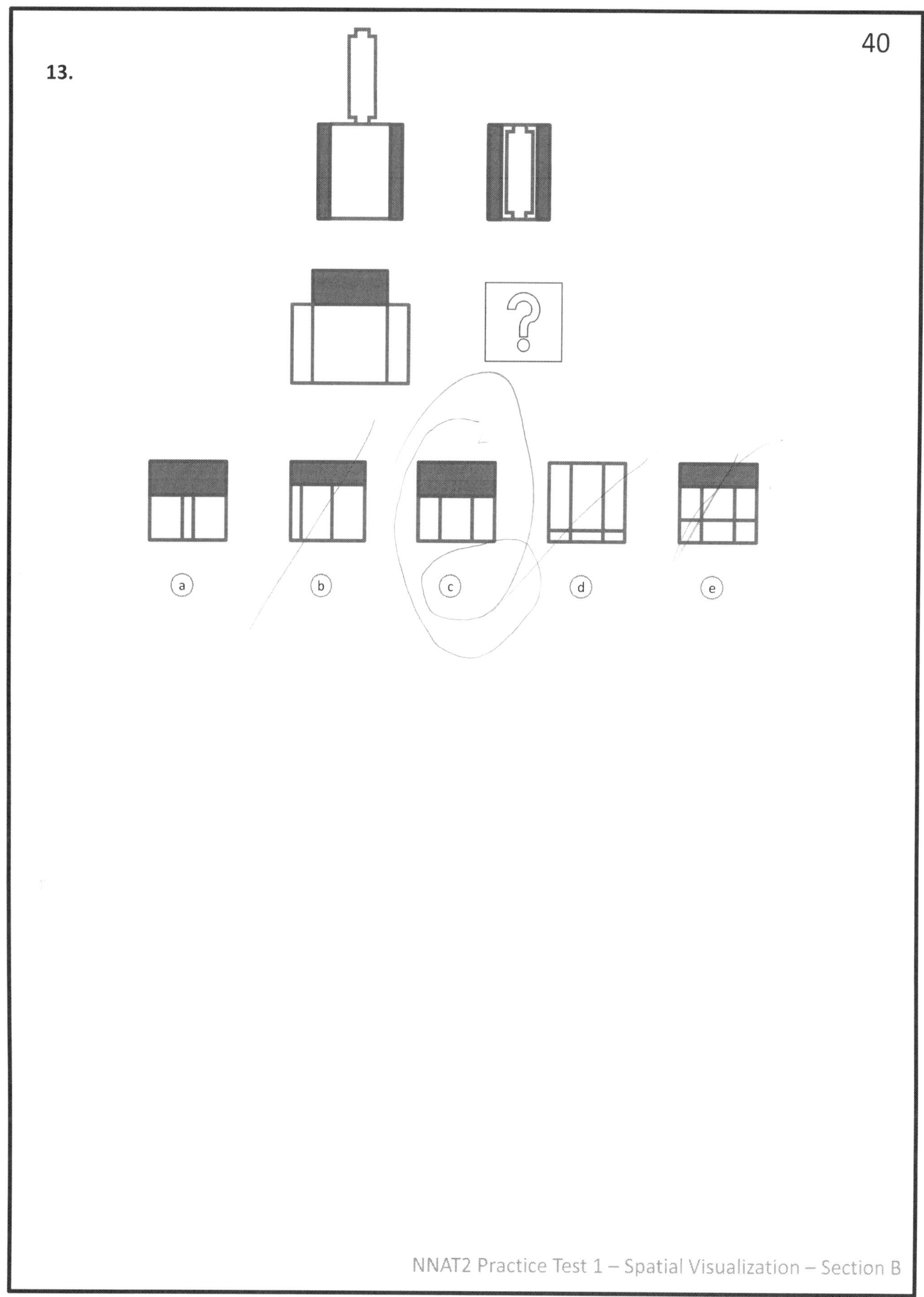

Practice Test 2 for the NNAT®2

Naglieri Nonverbal Ability Test®

Level D (Grades 3 & 4)

PATTERN COMPLETION

Each question in this section has a large rectangle with a picture or design. Within the large rectangle, there is a smaller rectangle with a question mark covering a section of the big rectangle. Pick the hidden part of the big rectangle and color the bubble under your choice.

1.

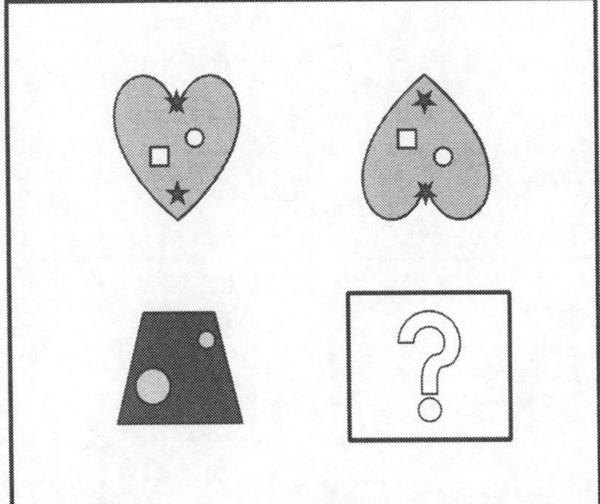

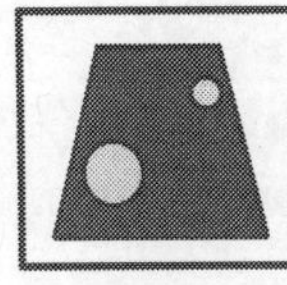

a b  d 

2.

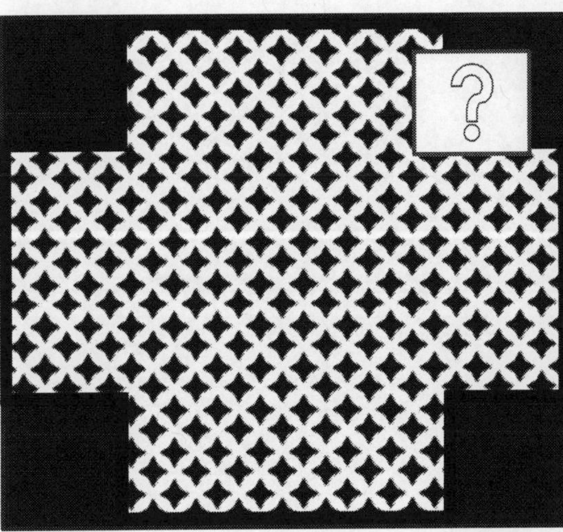

 b c d e

3.

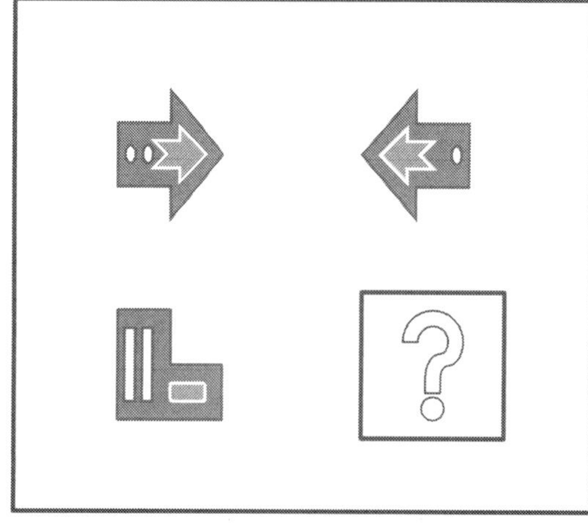

a

b

c

d

e

4.

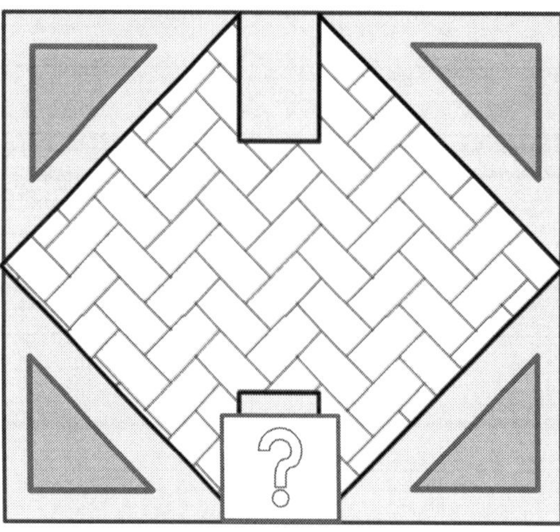

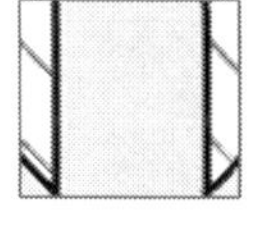
a

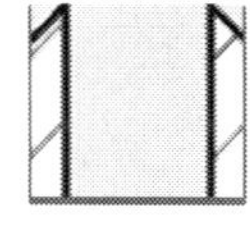
b

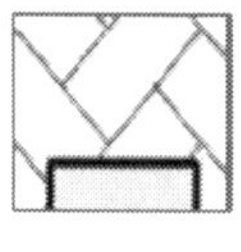
c

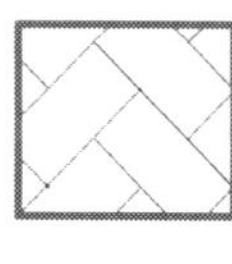
d

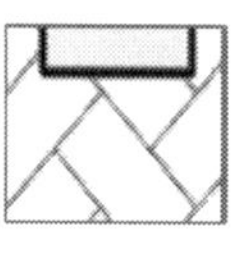
e

5.

a

b

c

d

e

6.

a

b

c

d

e

7.

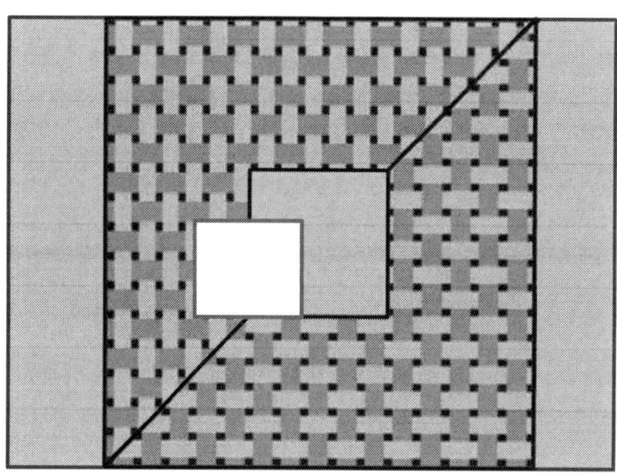

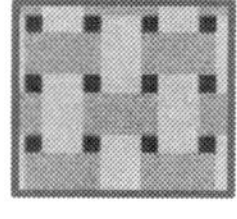
a

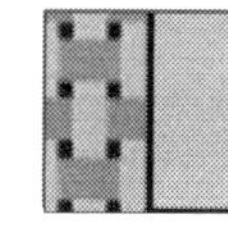
b

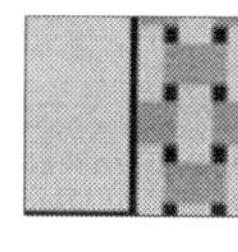
c

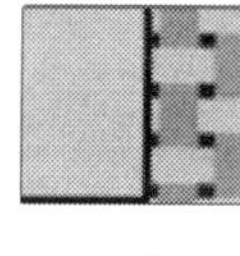
d

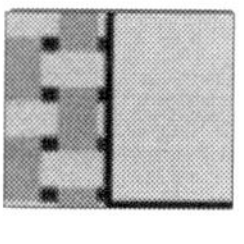
e

8.

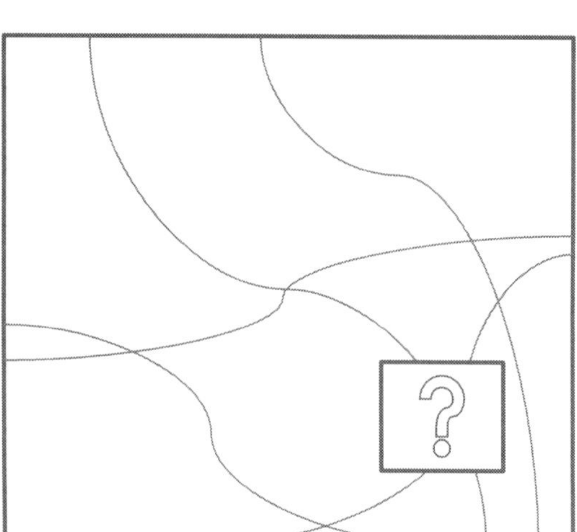

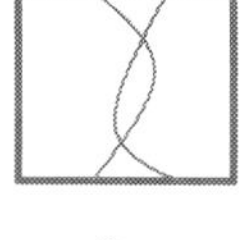
a

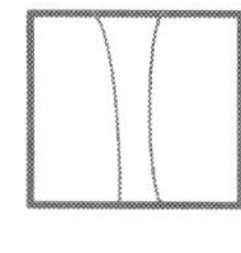
b

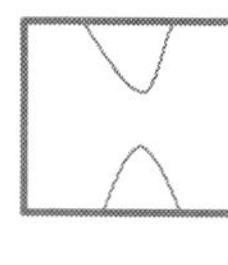
c

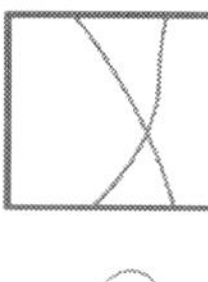
d

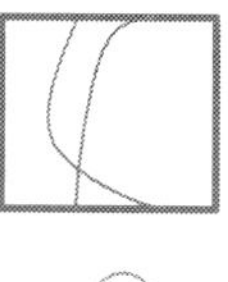
e

9.

a b c d e

10.

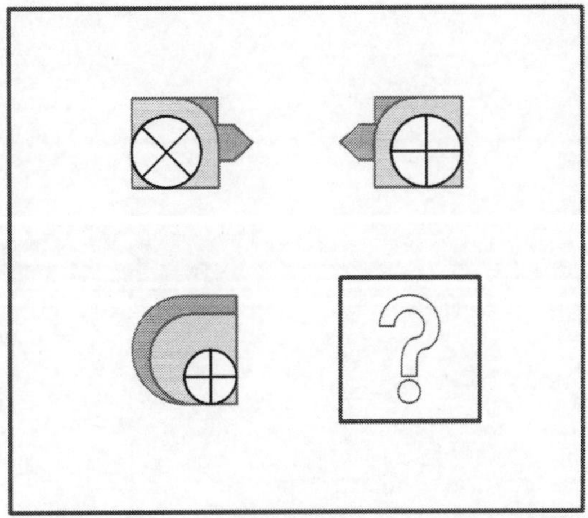

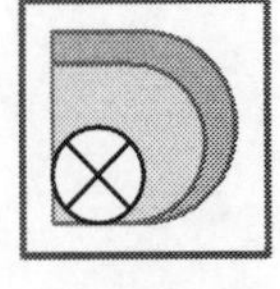

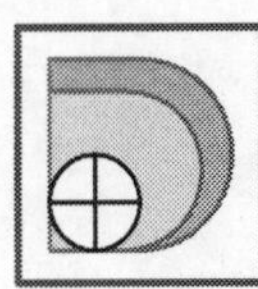
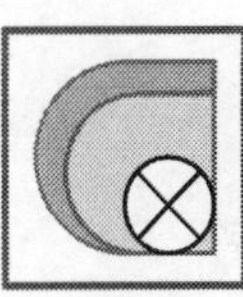

a b c d e

REASONING BY ANALOGY

Each question in this section has three rows of pictures. In each row, determine how the picture changes as you go across the row. The same changes should be echoed across all the three rows. Pick the missing picture and color the bubble under your choice.

1.

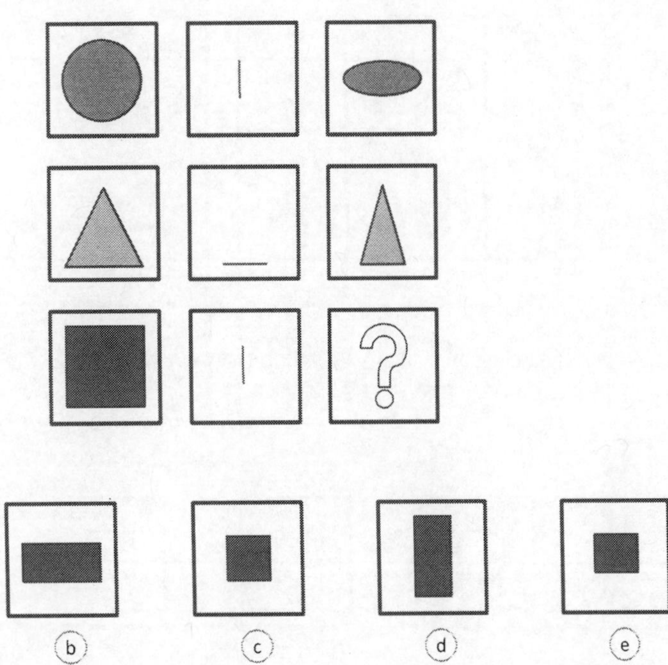

2.

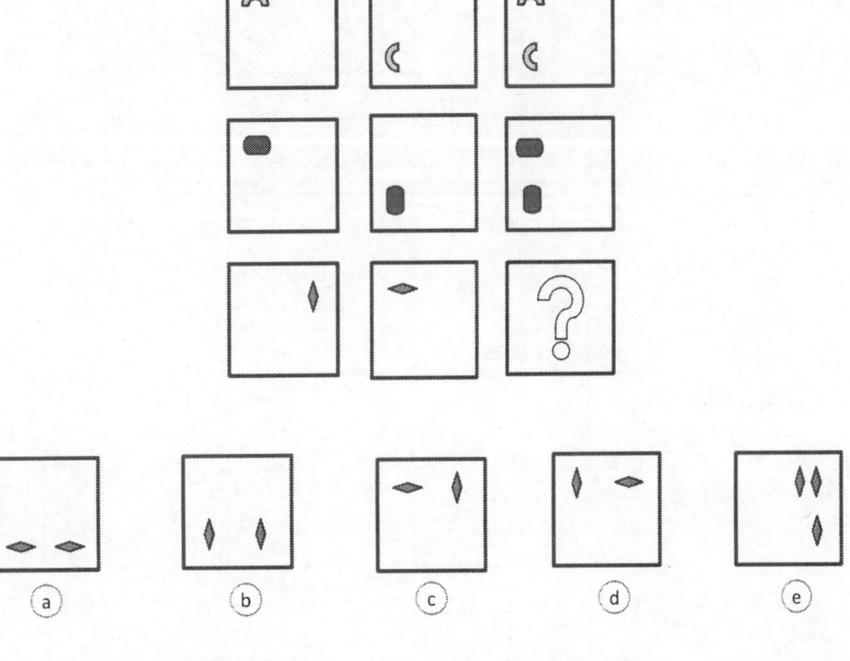

3.

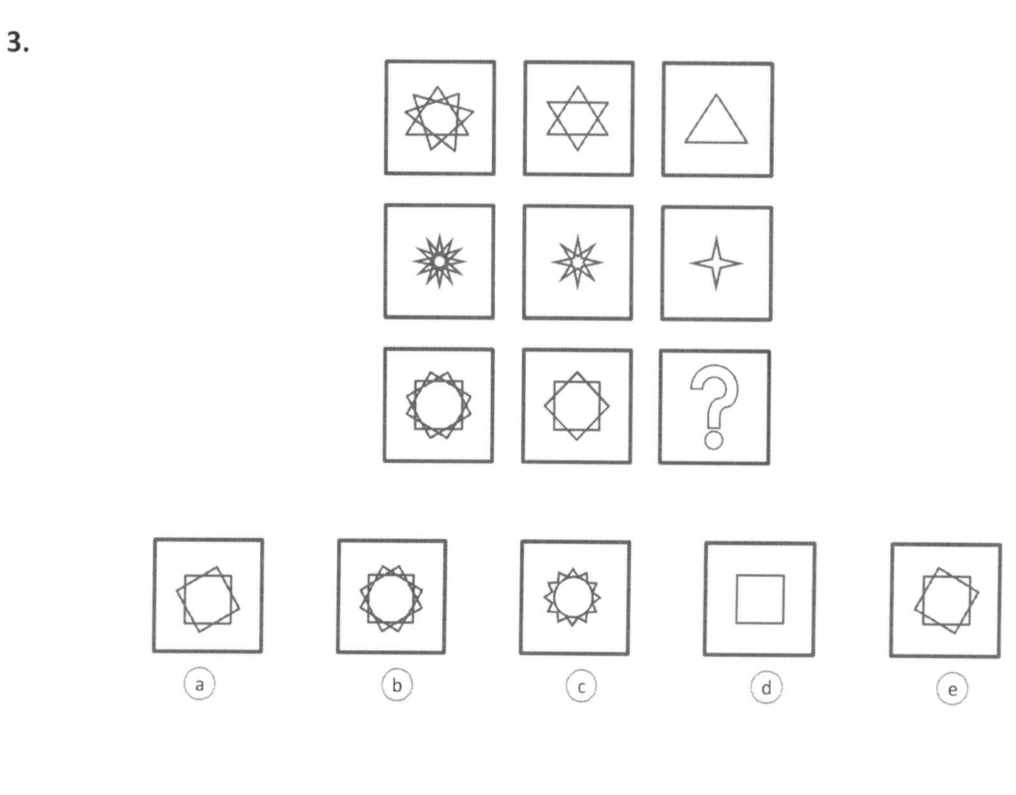

4.

5.

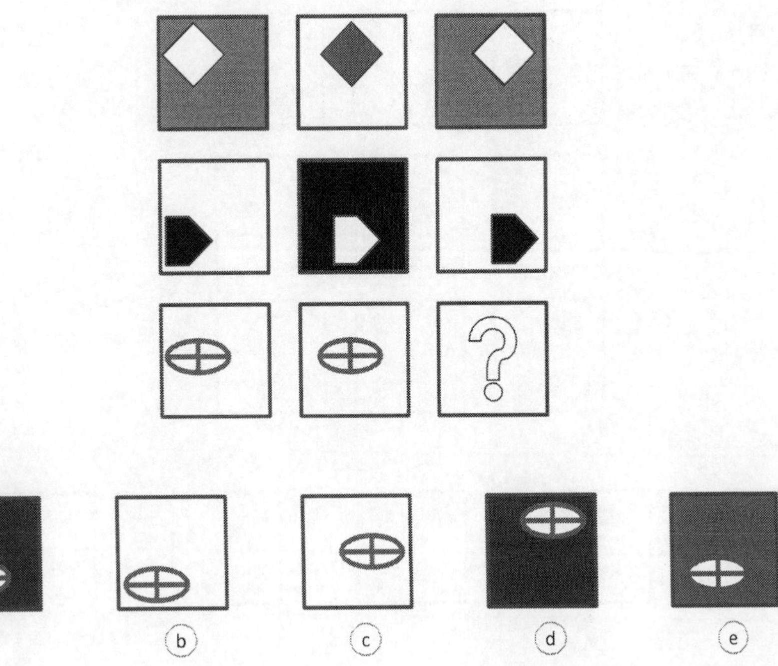

6.

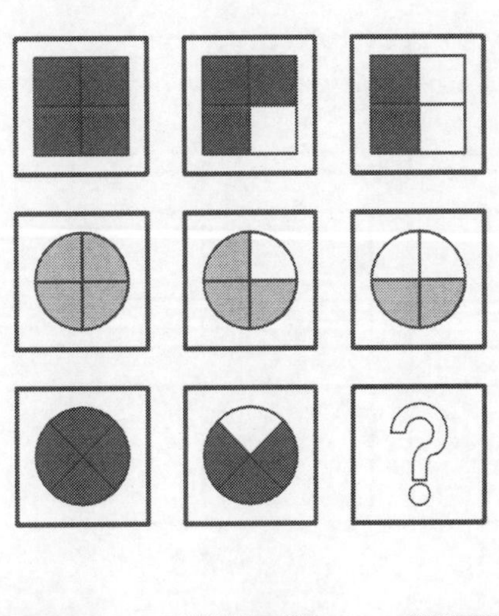

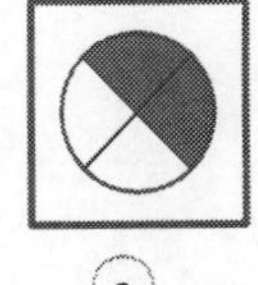

a

b

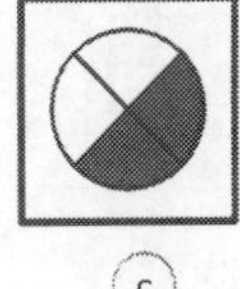

c

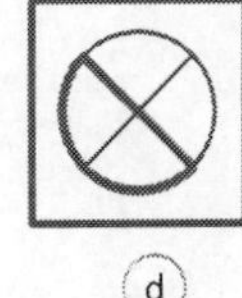

d

e

7.

8.

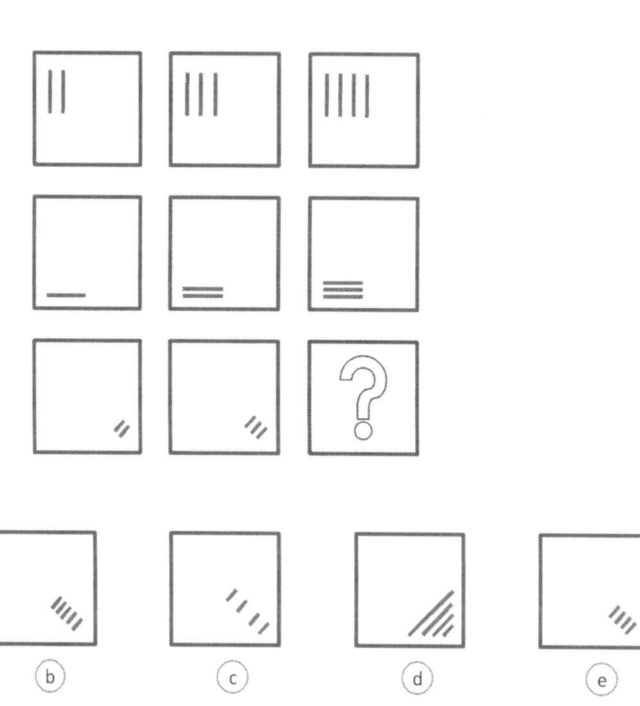

9.

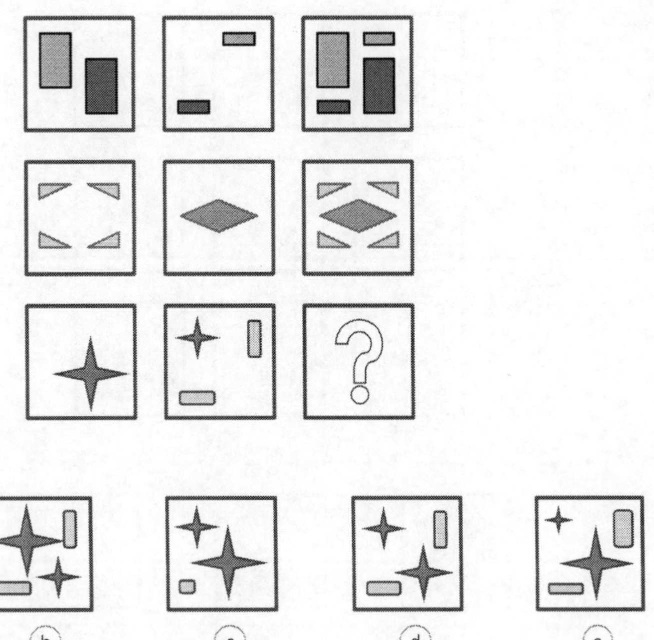

10.

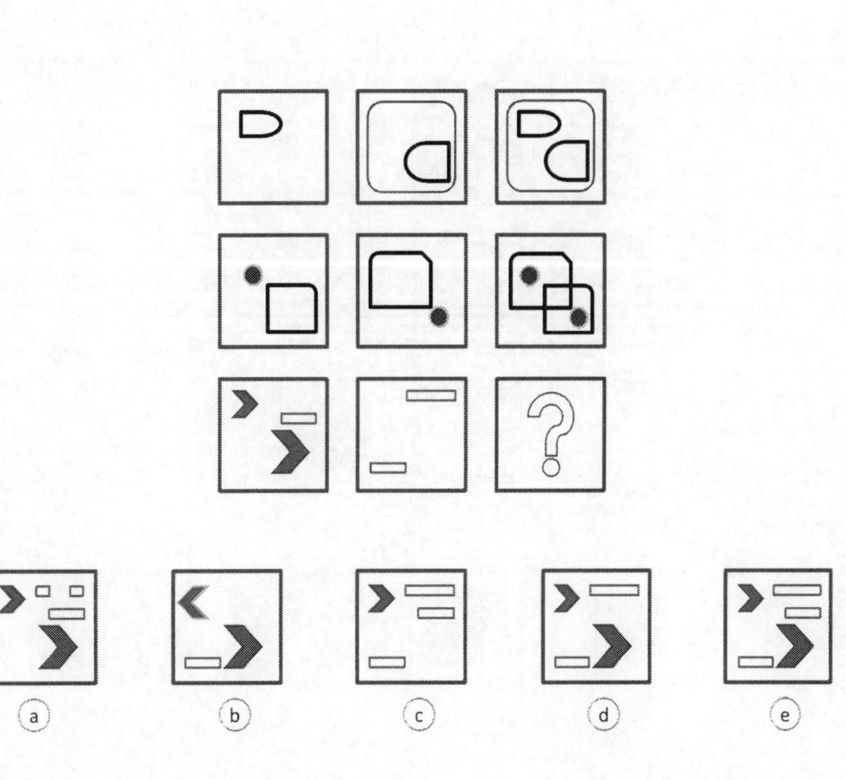

11.

12.

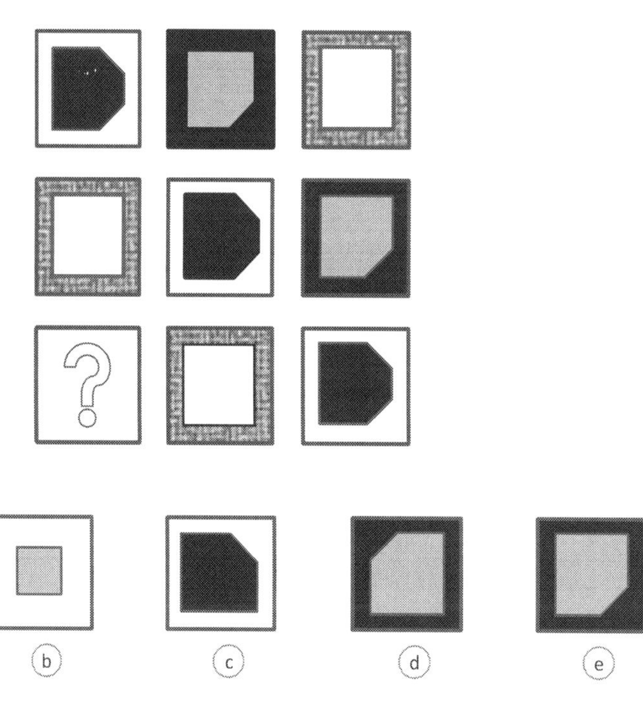

13.

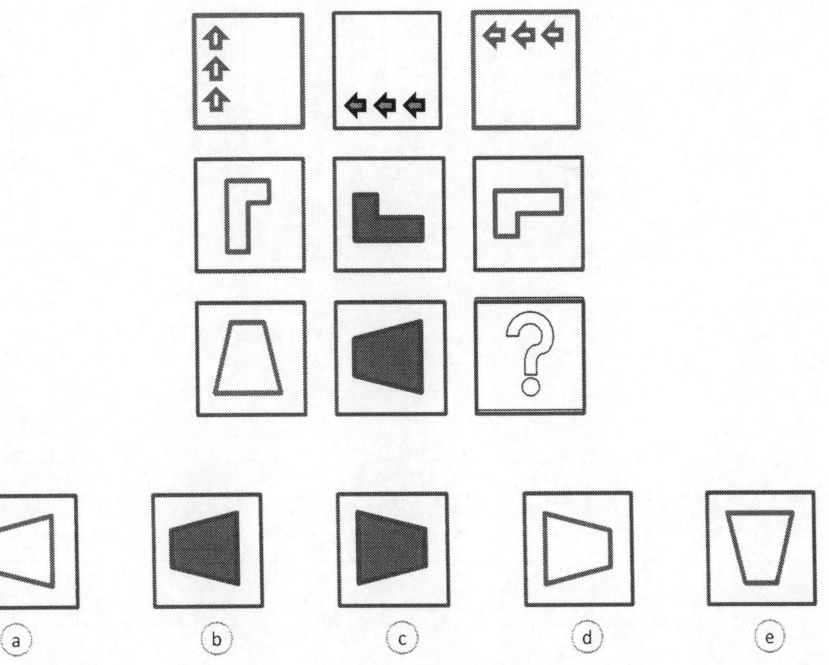

14.

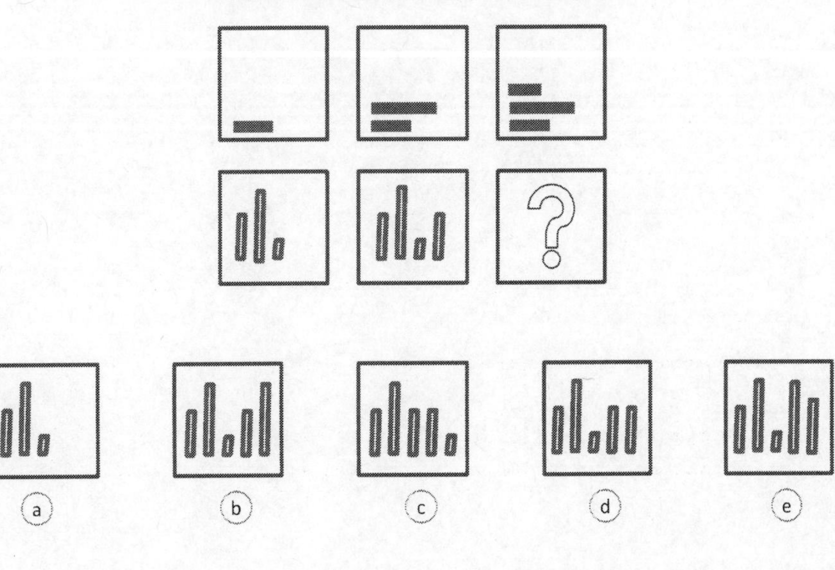

SERIAL REASONING

Each question in this section has a matrix of three rows and three columns. The pictures change as you go across the row and down the column in the matrix. Determine the change pattern within the matrix and pick the correct missing picture that will complete the matrix. Color the bubble under your choice.

1.

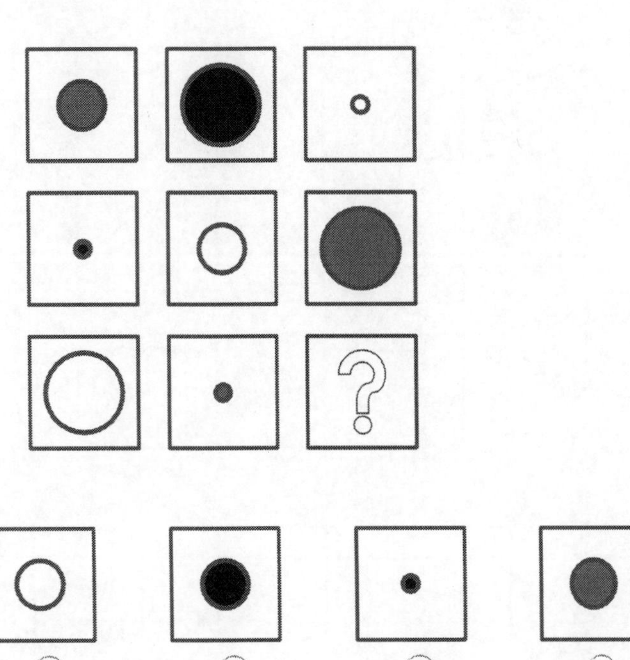

(a) (b) (c) (d) (e)

2.

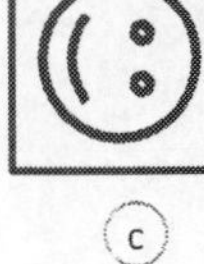

(a) (b) (c) (d) (e)

3.

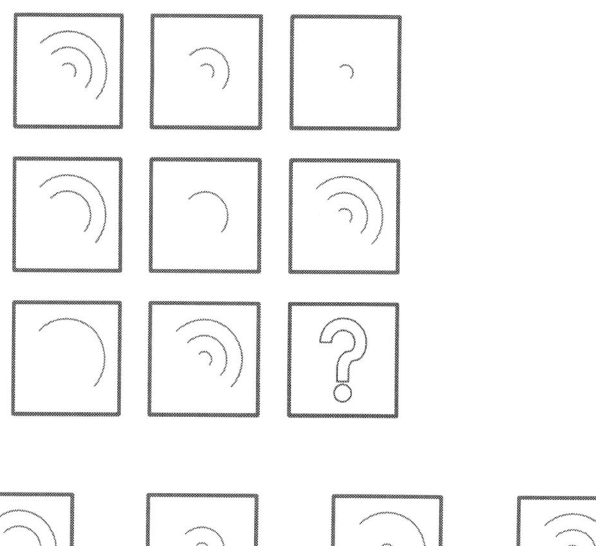

4.

5.

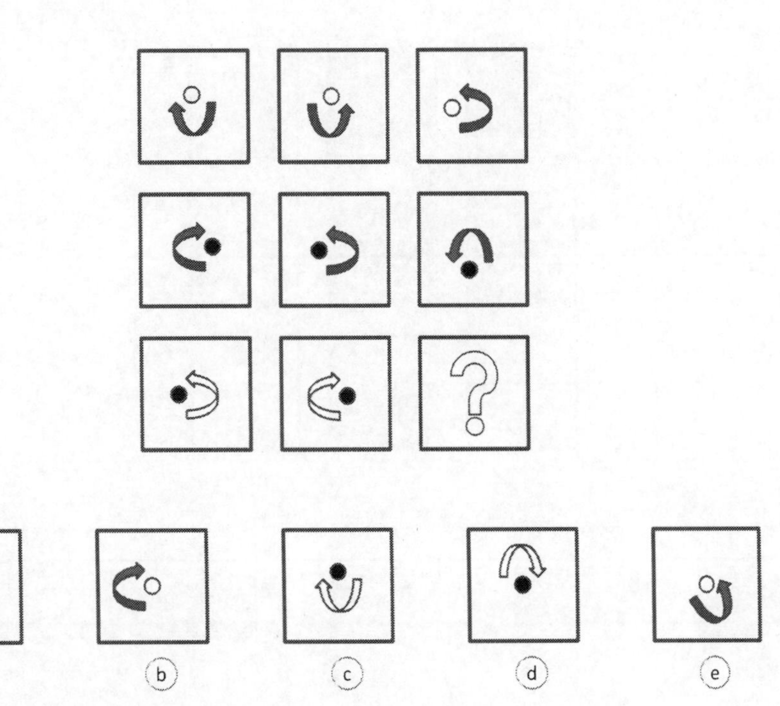

6.

7.

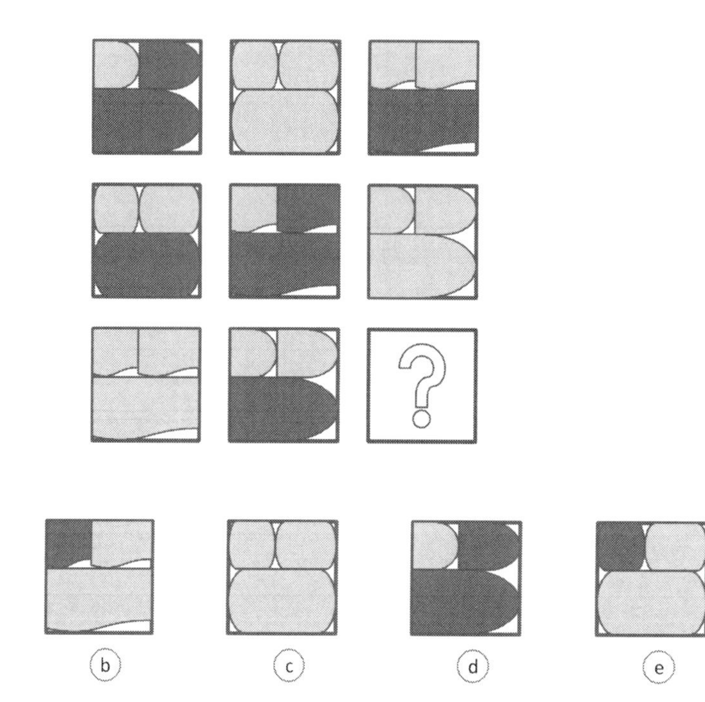

8.

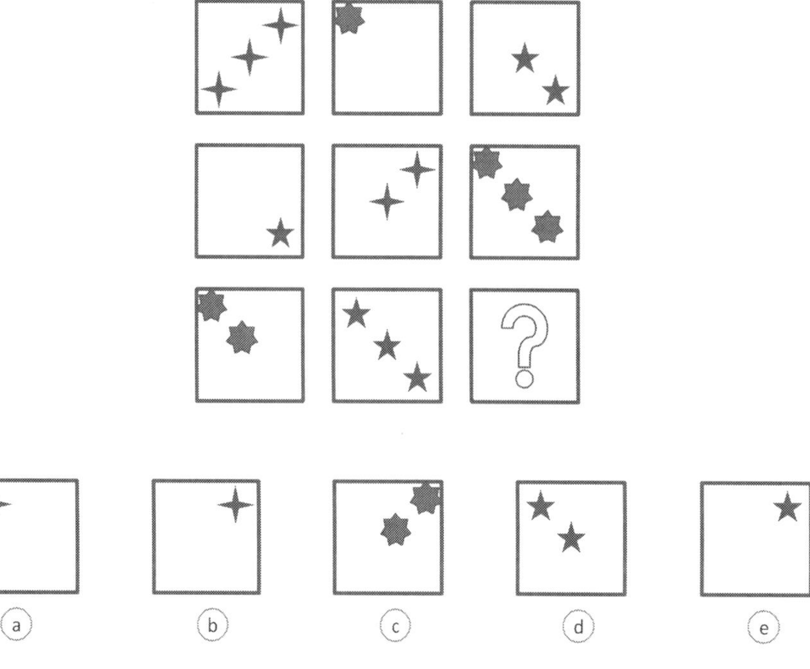

9.

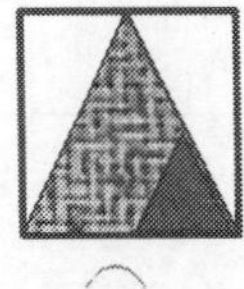
a

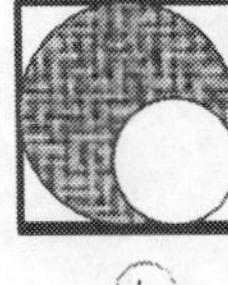
b

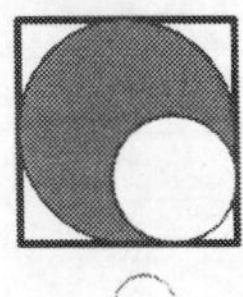
c

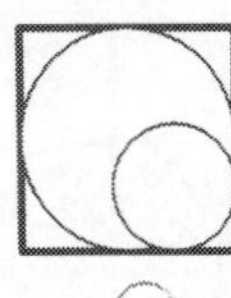
d

e

10.

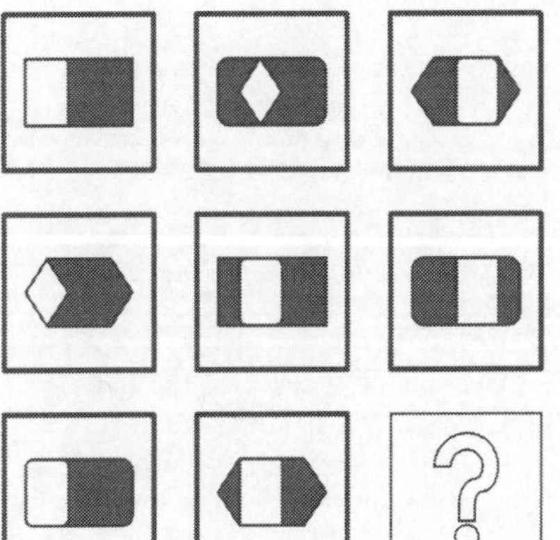

a

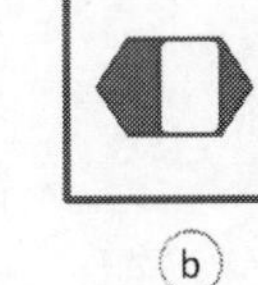
b

c

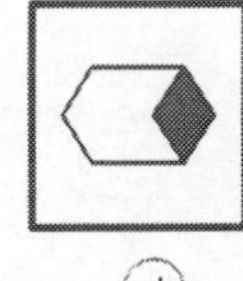
d

e

11.

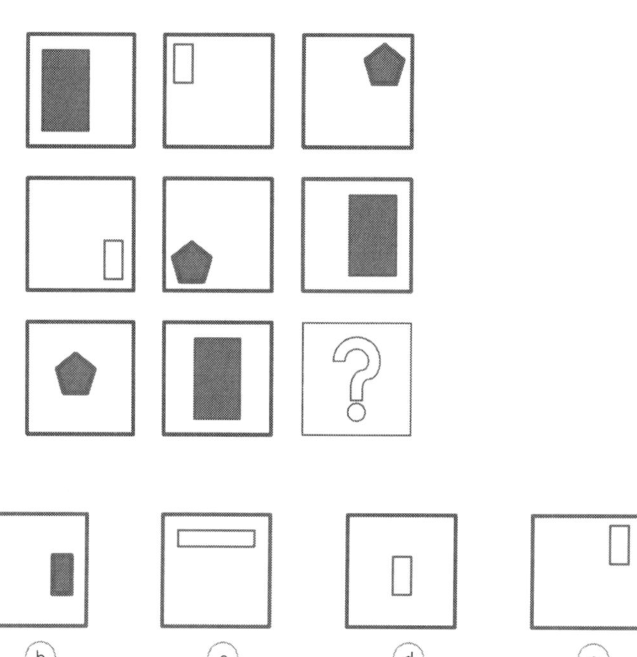

SPATIAL VISUALIZATION – SECTION A

Each question in this section has three pictures on the top row. The third picture in the row is formed by combining the first two pictures. Using the same principle, pick the missing picture in the bottom row. Color the bubble under your choice.

1.

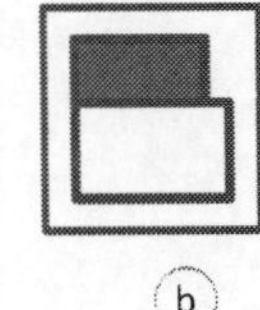
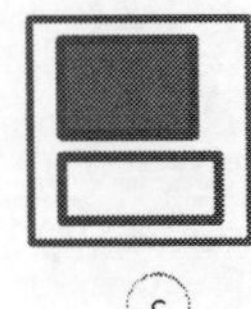

a b c d e

2.

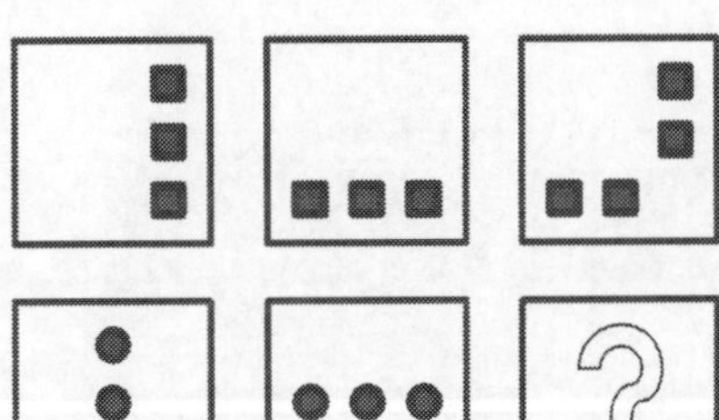

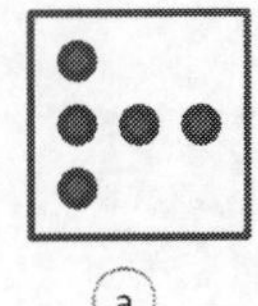
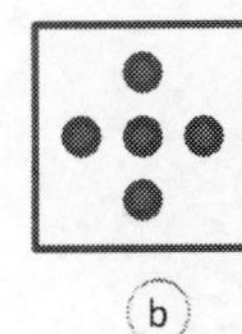
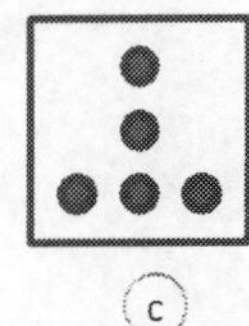
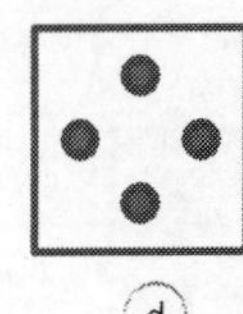
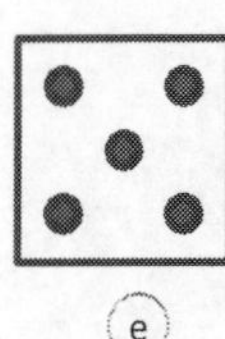

a b c d e

3.

a

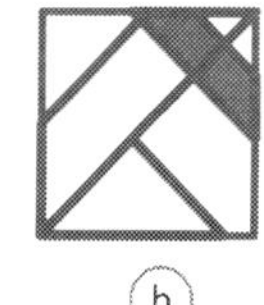
b

c

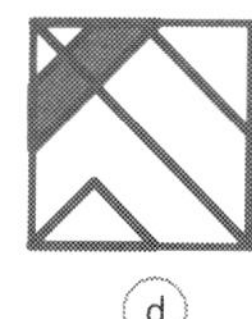
d

e

4.

a

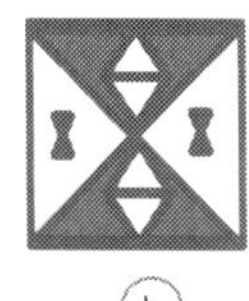
b

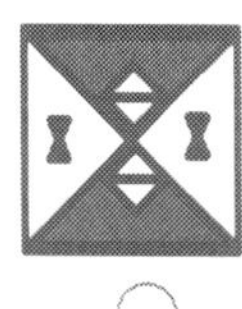
c

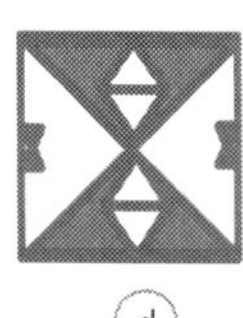
d

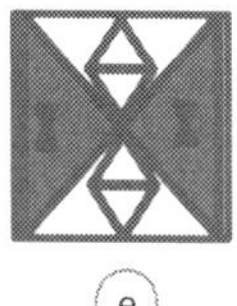
e

5.

a

b

c

d

e

6.

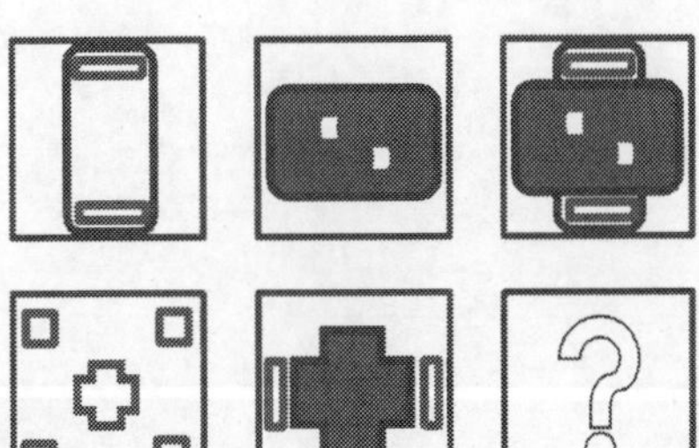

a

b

c

d

e

SPATIAL VISUALIZATION – SECTION B

Each question in this section has two pictures on the top row. The picture on the right in the top row is created by folding the outside shapes into the main shape of the picture on the left. Now, pick the picture that would be created when the outside shapes in the second row are folded in the same manner as the first row. Color the bubble under your choice.

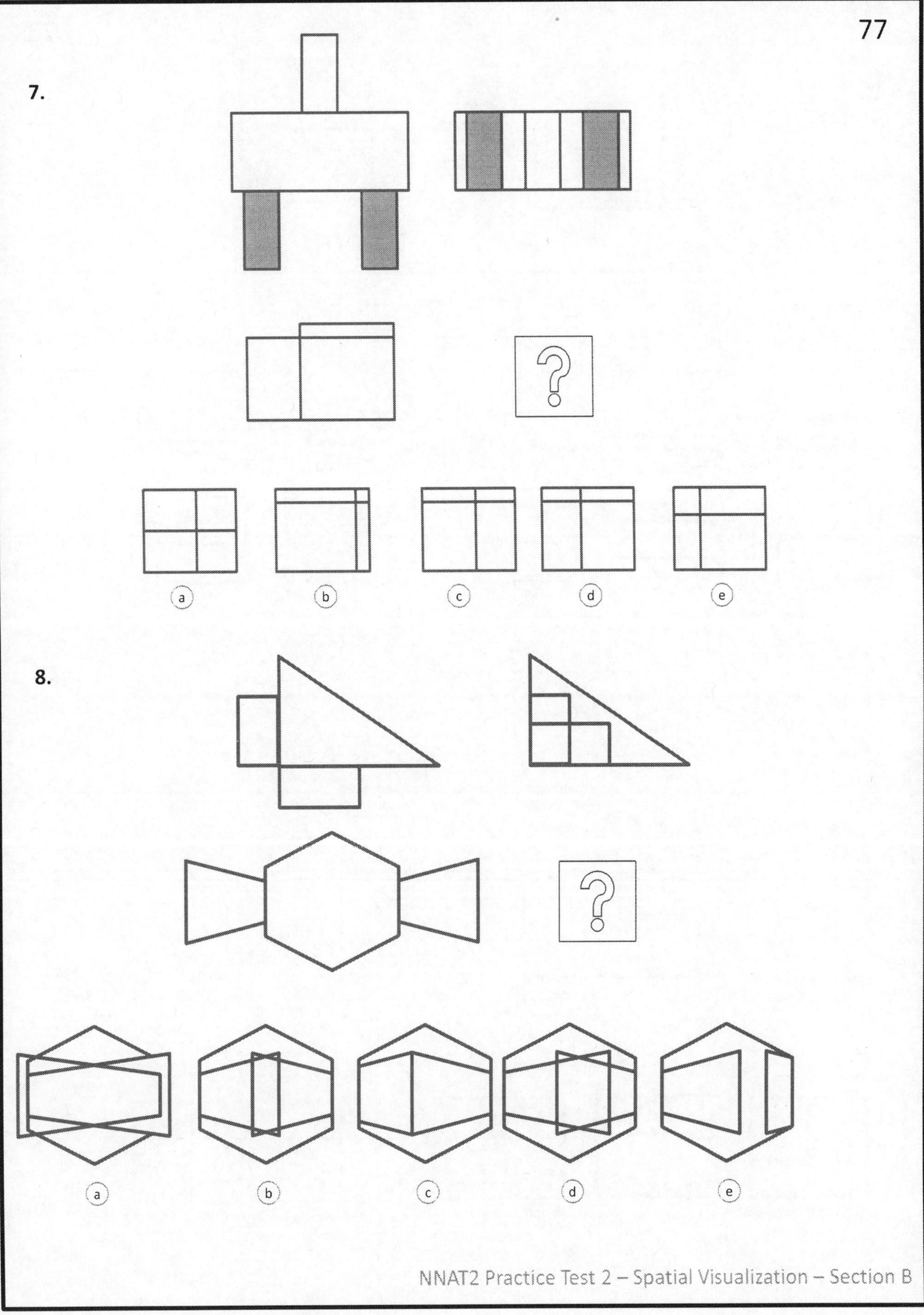
7.
a
b
c
d
e
8.
a
b
c
d
e

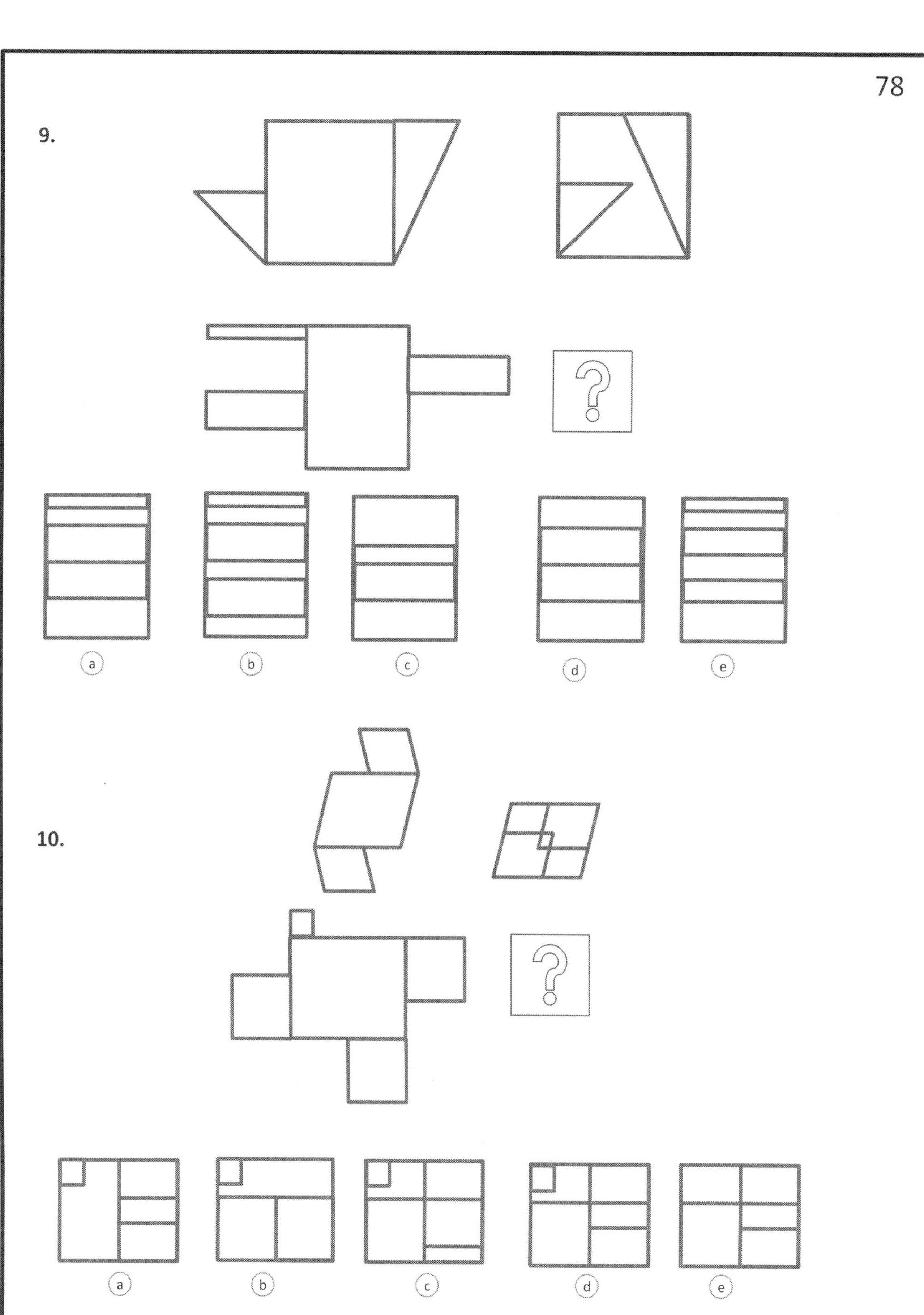
9.
a
b
c
d
e
10.
a
b
c
d
e

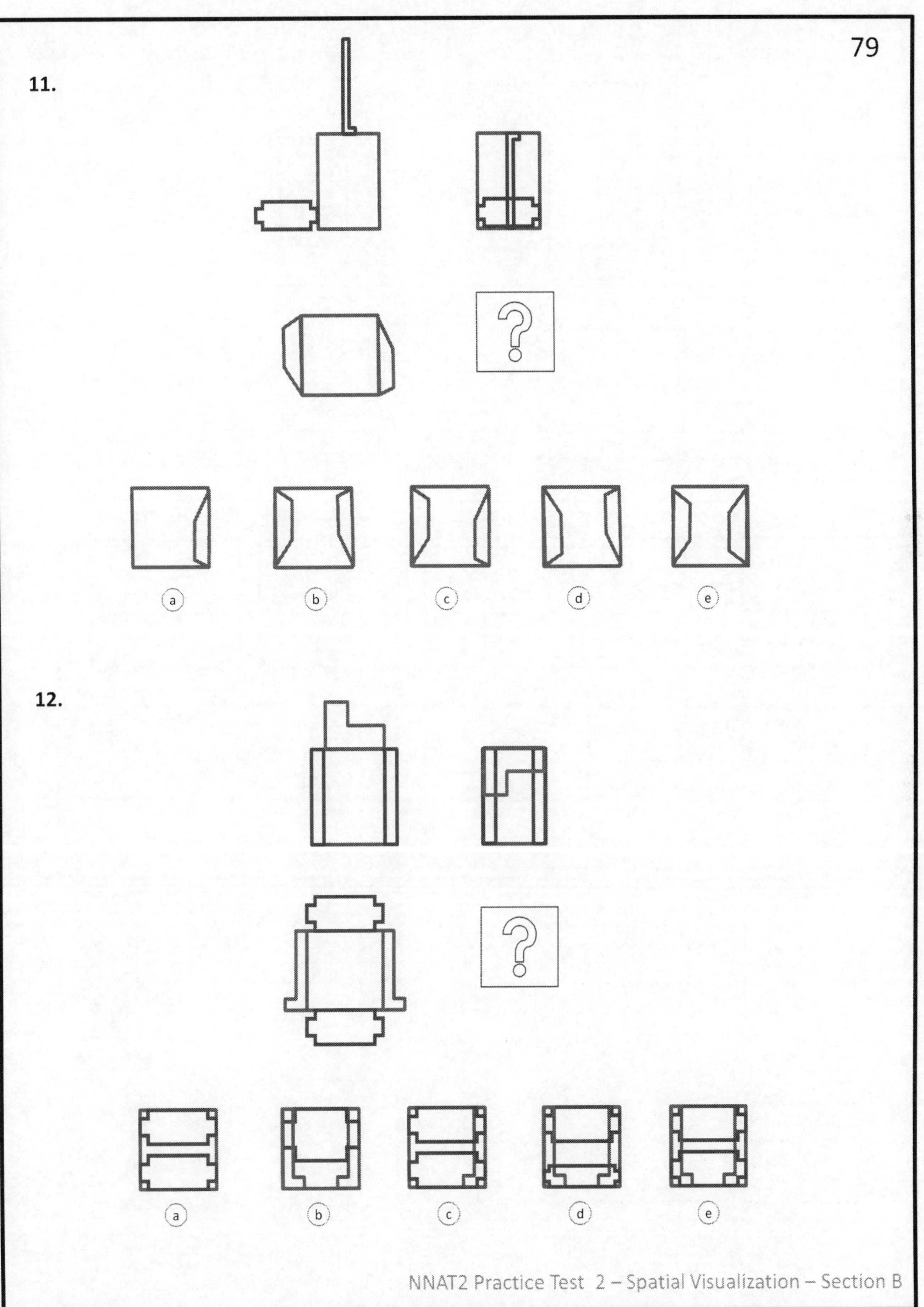
11.
a
b
c
d
e
12.
a
b
c
d
e

13.

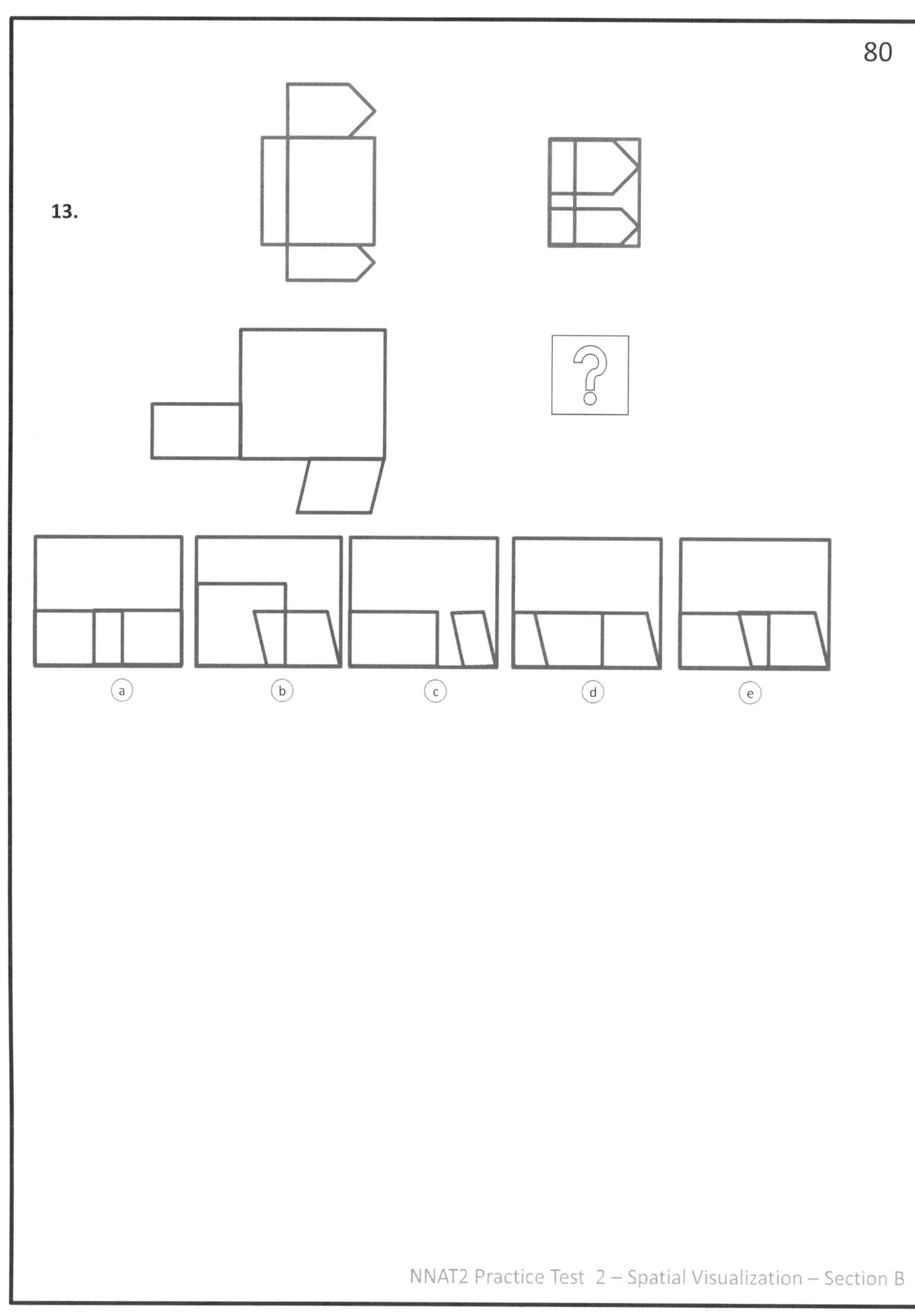

Practice Test 3 for the NNAT®2

Naglieri Nonverbal Ability Test®

Level D (Grades 3 & 4)

PATTERN COMPLETION

Each question in this section has a large rectangle with a picture or design. Within the large rectangle, there is a smaller rectangle with a question mark covering a section of the big rectangle. Pick the hidden part of the big rectangle and color the bubble under your choice.

1.

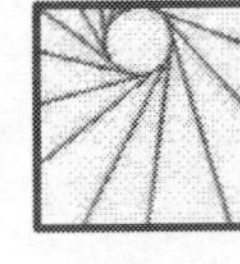

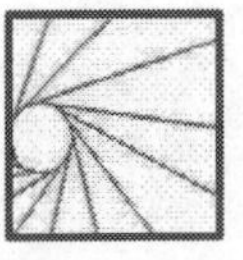

(a) (b) (c) (d) (e)

2.

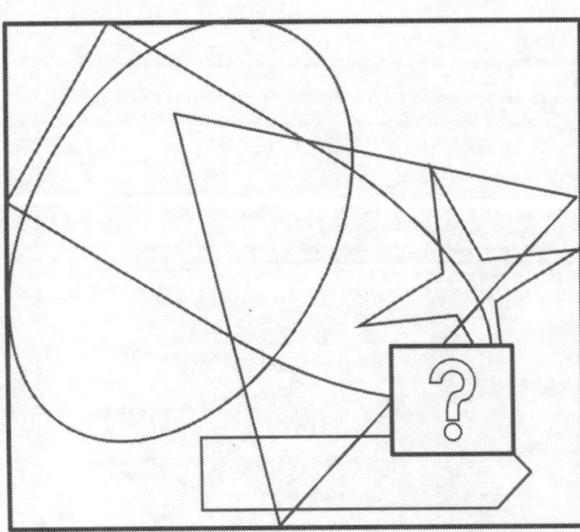

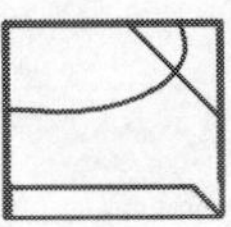
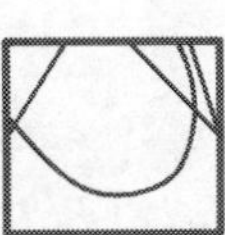

(a) (b) (c) (d) (e)

3.

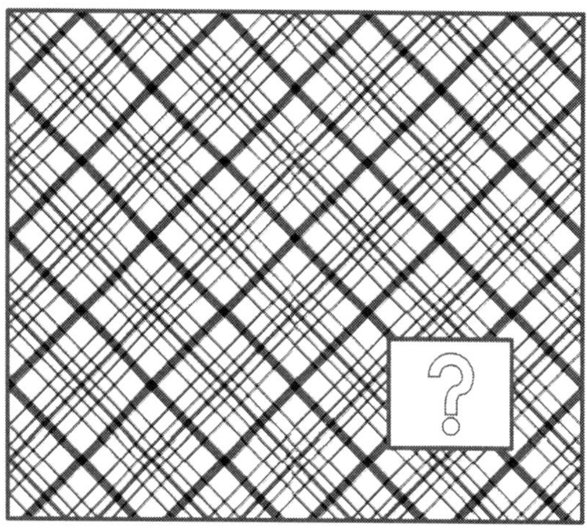

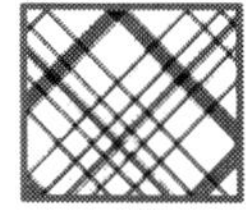

a

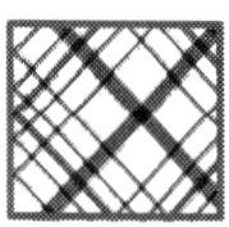

b

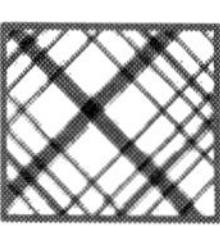

c

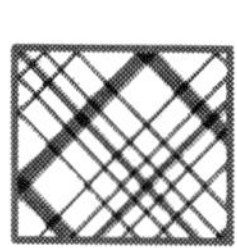

d

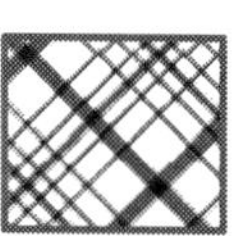

e

4.

a

b

c

d

e

5.

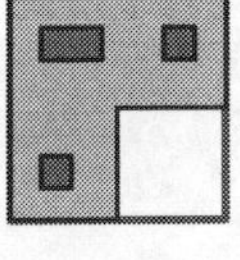

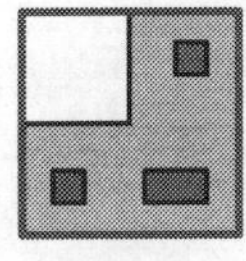

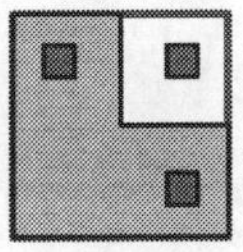

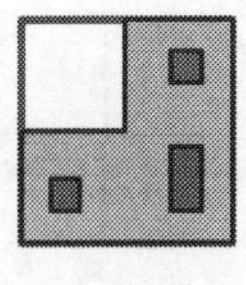

a b c d e

6.

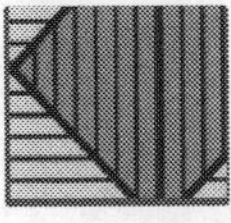

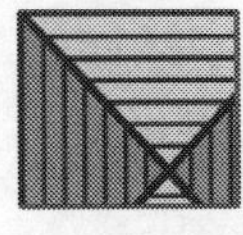

a b c d e

7.

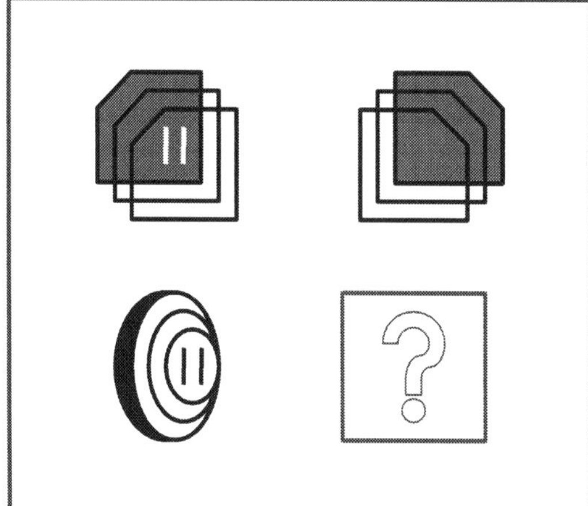

a b c d e

8.

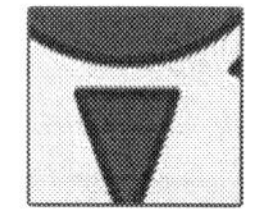

a b c d e

9.

a

b

c

d

e

10.

a

b

c

d

e

REASONING BY ANALOGY

Each question in this section has three rows of pictures. In each row, determine how the picture changes as you go across the row. The same changes should be echoed across all the three rows. Pick the missing picture and color the bubble under your choice.

1.

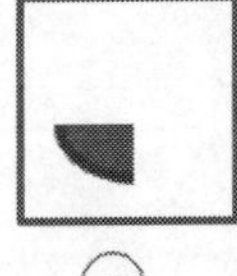
a

b

c

d

e

2.

a

b

c

d

e

3.

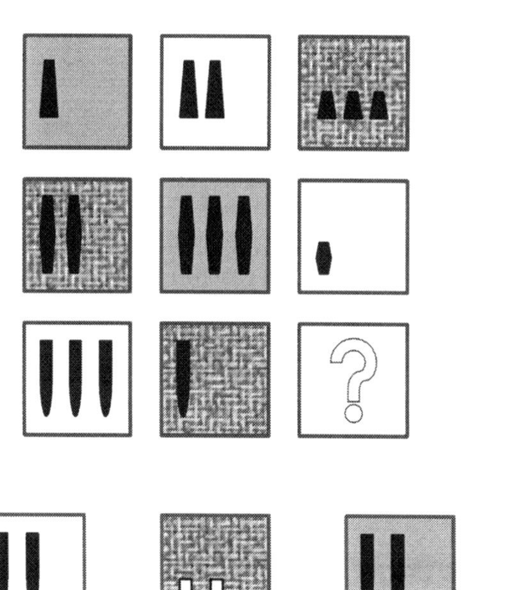

4.

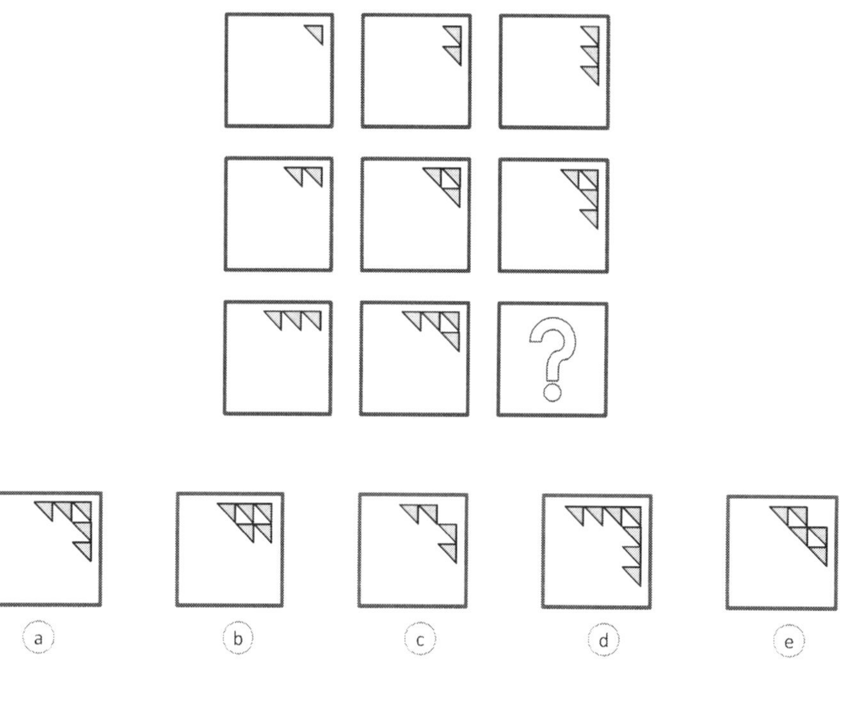

5.

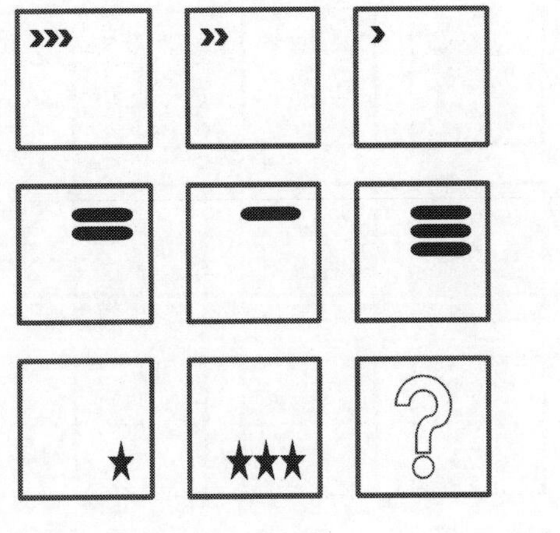

(a)

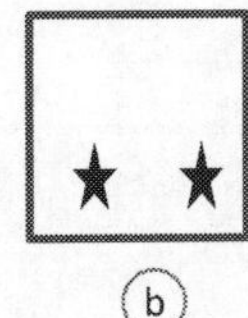
(b)

(c)

(d)

(e)

6.

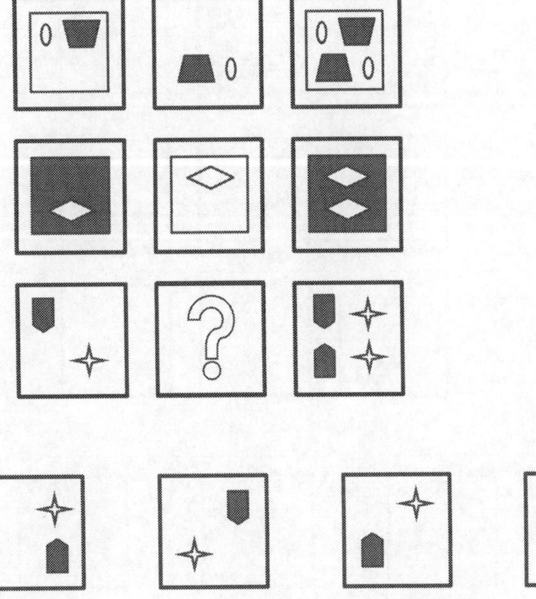

(a) (b) (c) (d) (e)

7.

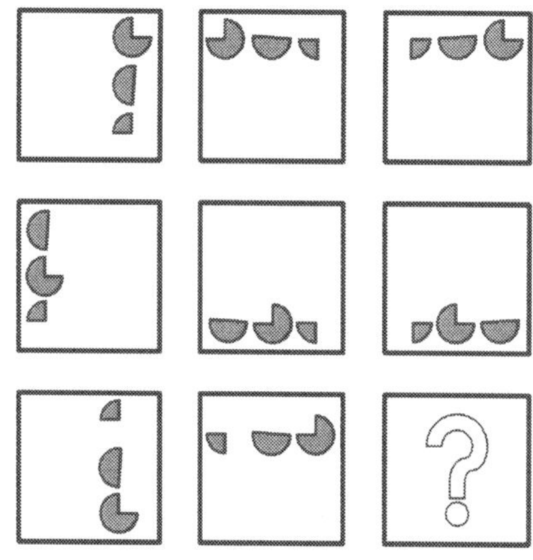

a

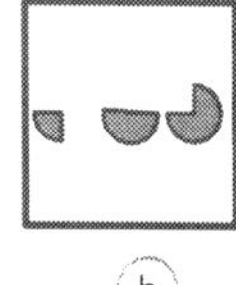

b

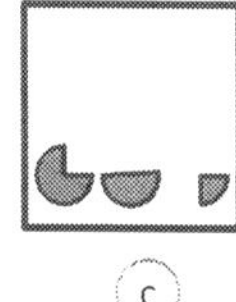

c

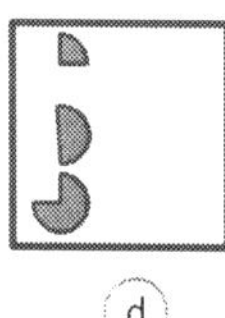

d

e

8.

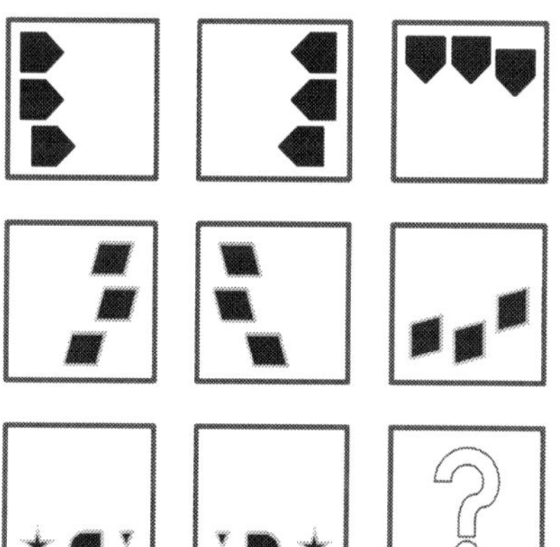

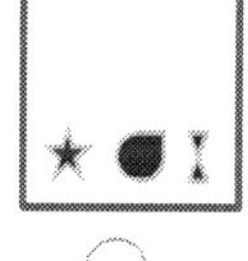

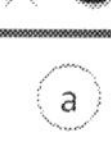

a

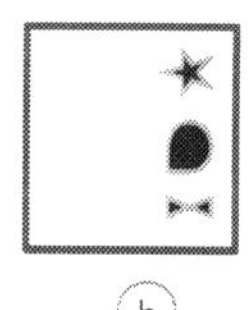

b

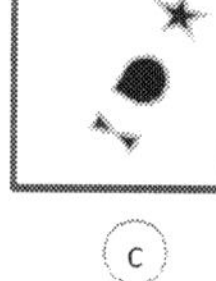

c

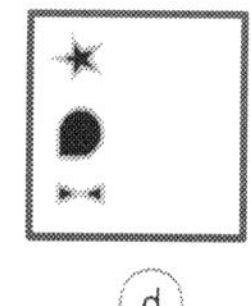

d

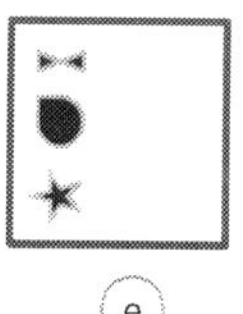

e

9.

a b c d e

10.

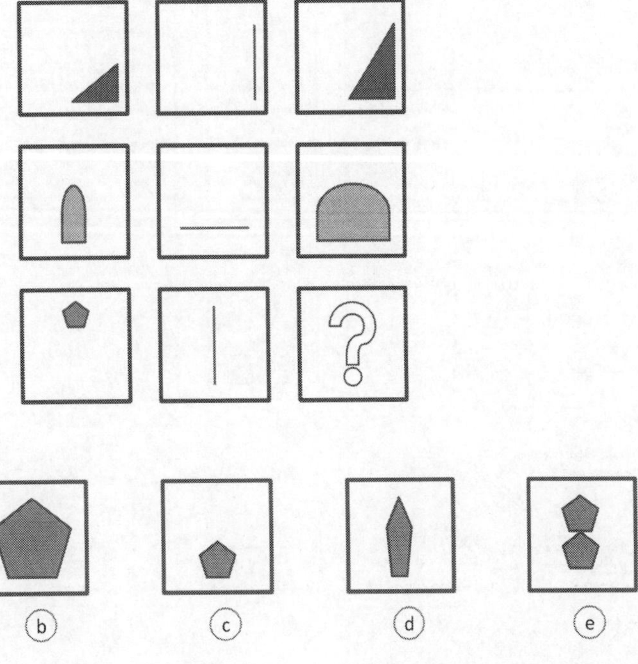

a b c d e

11.

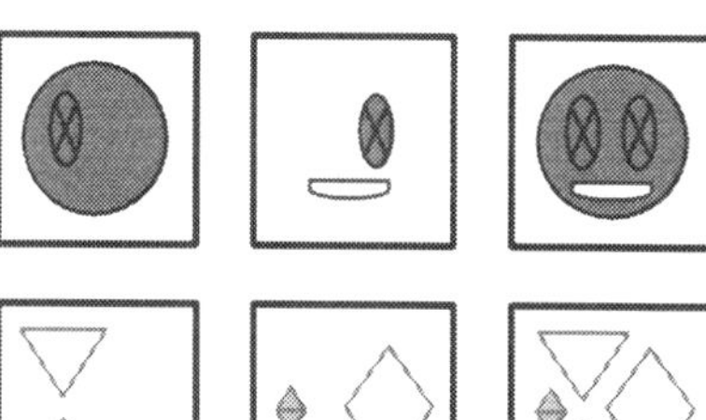

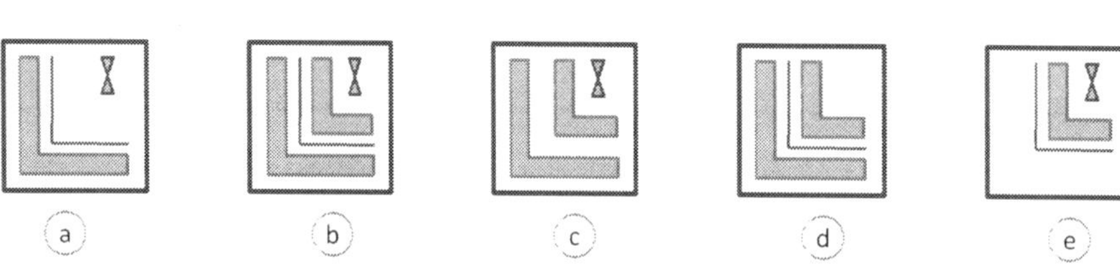

12.

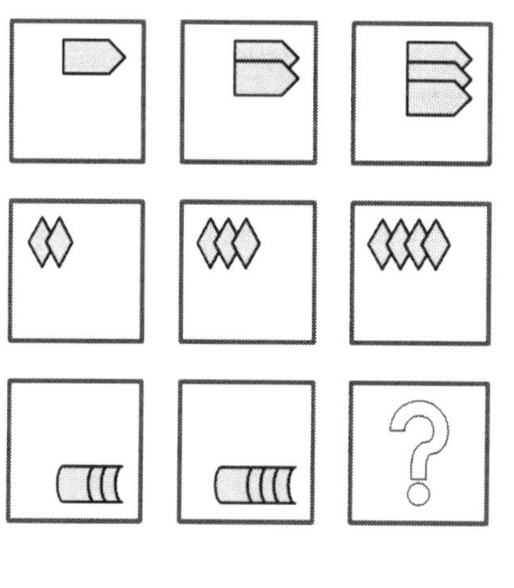

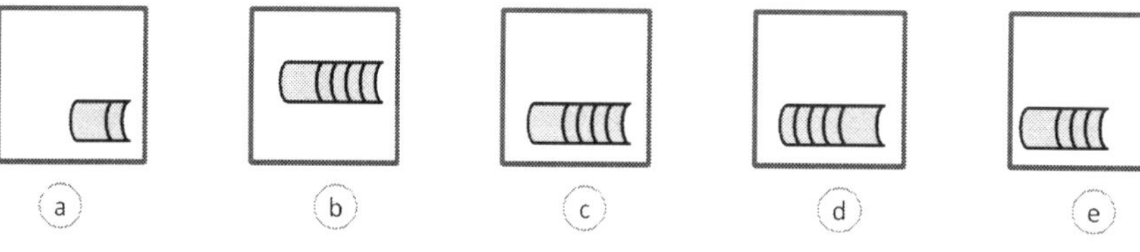

13.

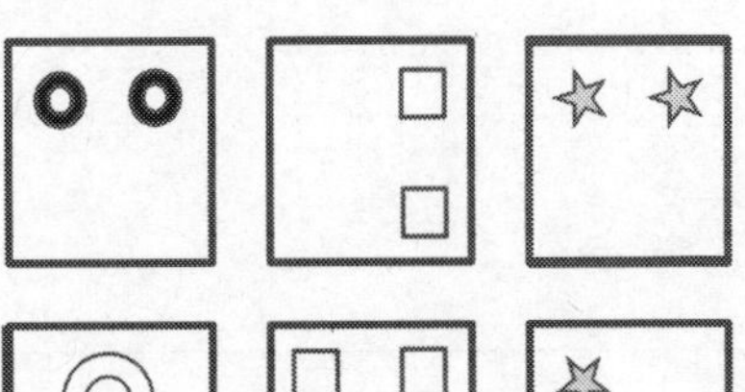
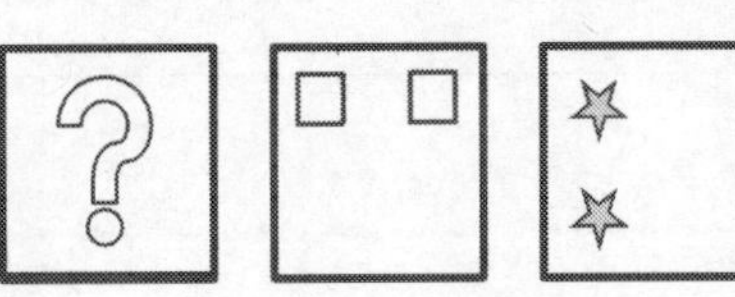
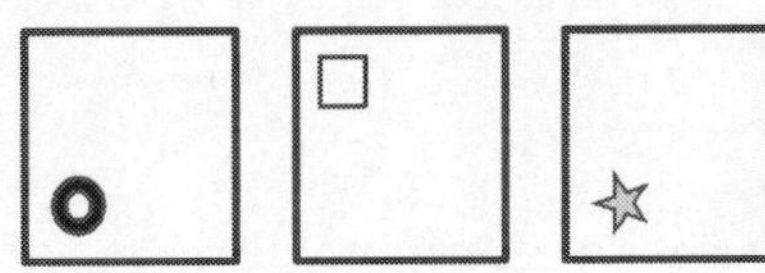

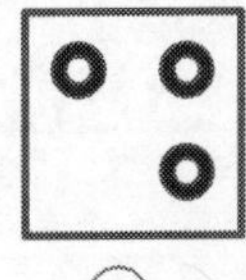
a

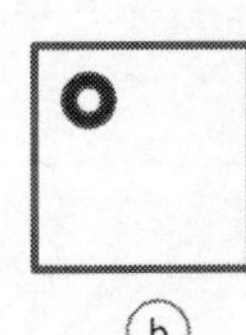
b

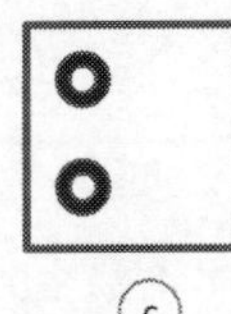
c

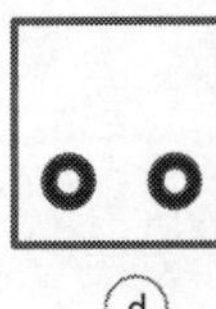
d

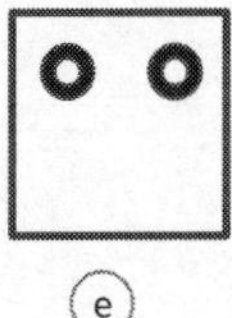
e

14.

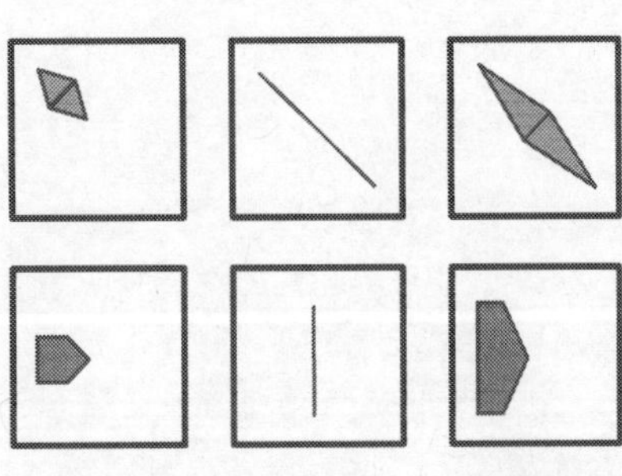

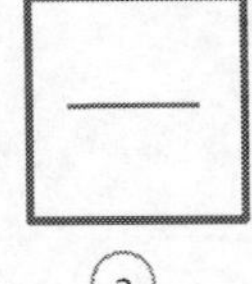
a

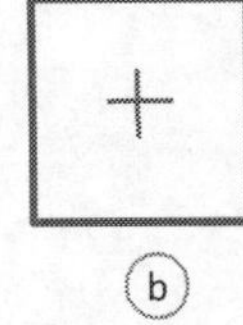
b

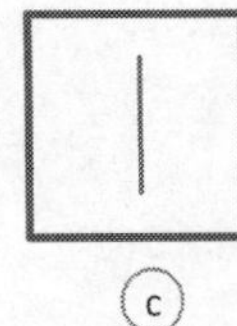
c

d

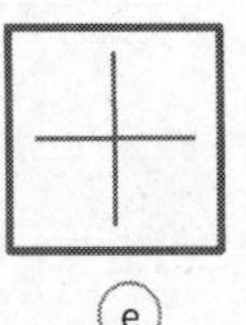
e

SERIAL REASONING

Each question in this section has a matrix of three rows and three columns. The pictures change as you go across the row and down the column in the matrix. Determine the change pattern within the matrix and pick the correct missing picture that will complete the matrix. Color the bubble under your choice.

1.

(a)

(b)

(c)

(d)

(e)

2.

(a)

(b)

(c)

(d)

(e)

3.

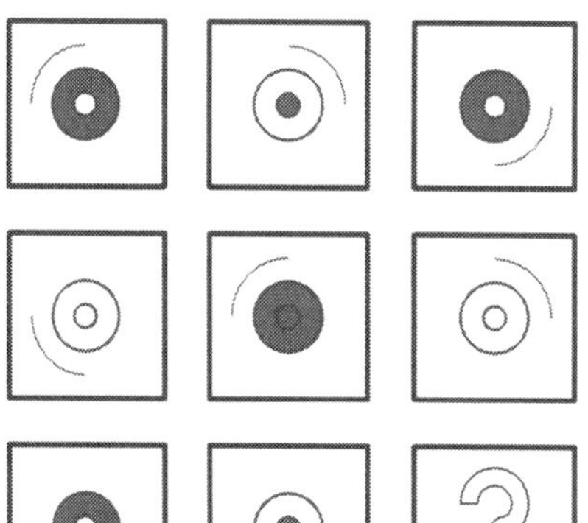

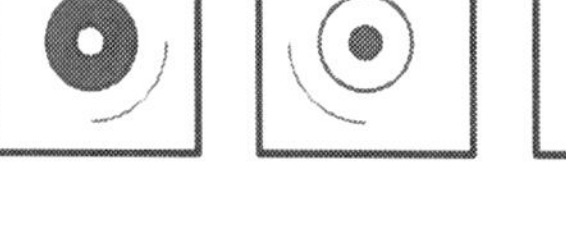

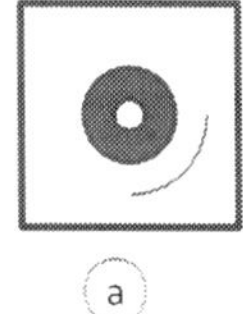

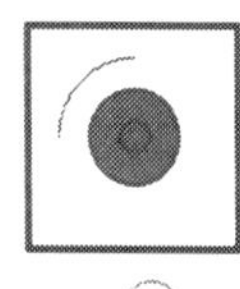

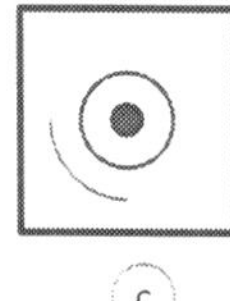

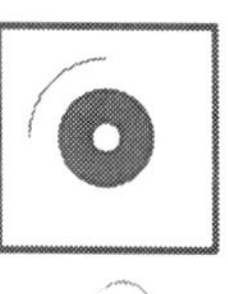

a b c d e

4.

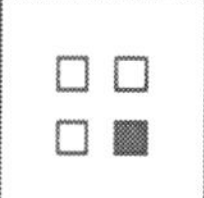

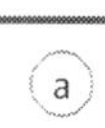

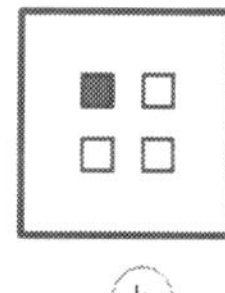

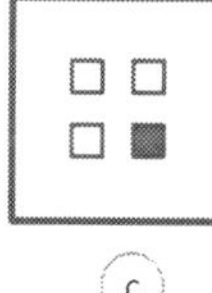

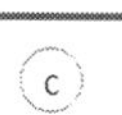

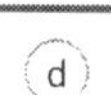

e

5.

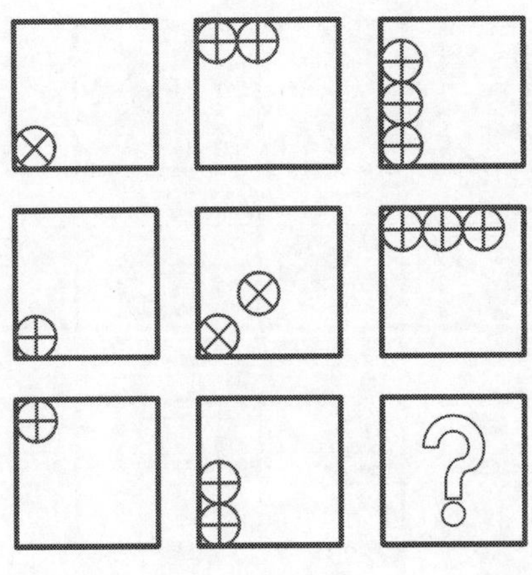

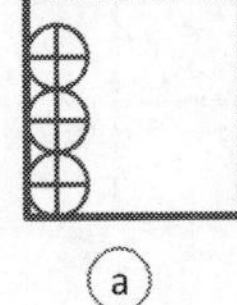

a

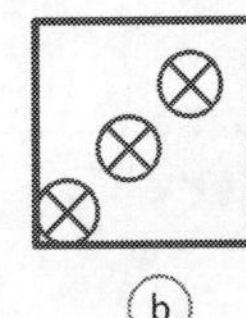

b

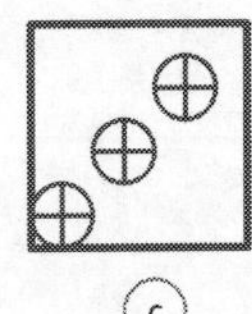

c

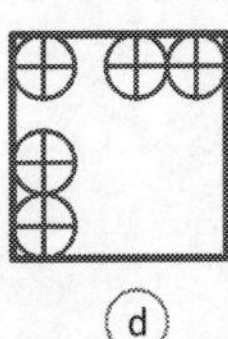

d

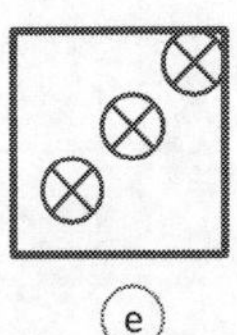

e

6.

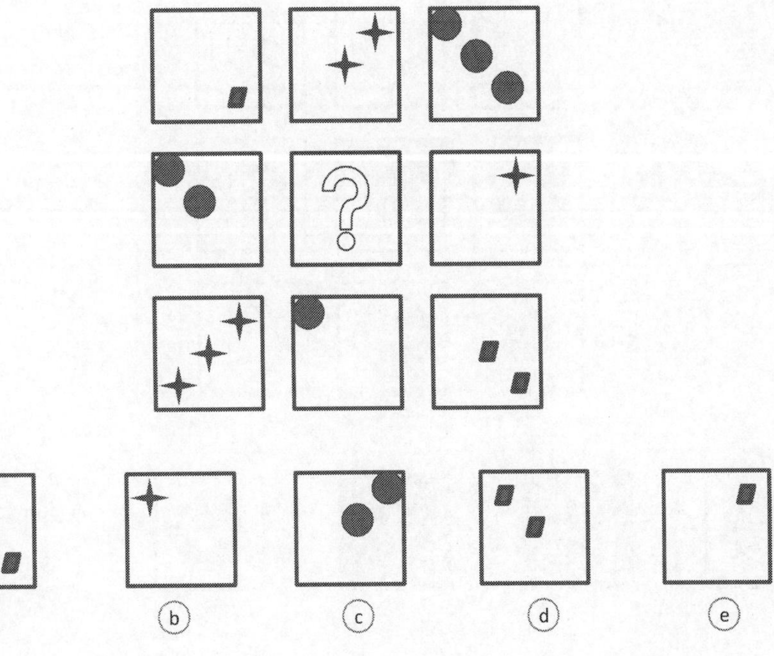

7.

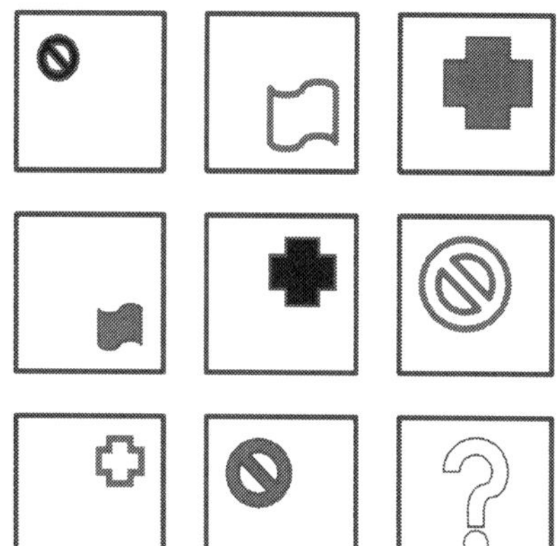

8.

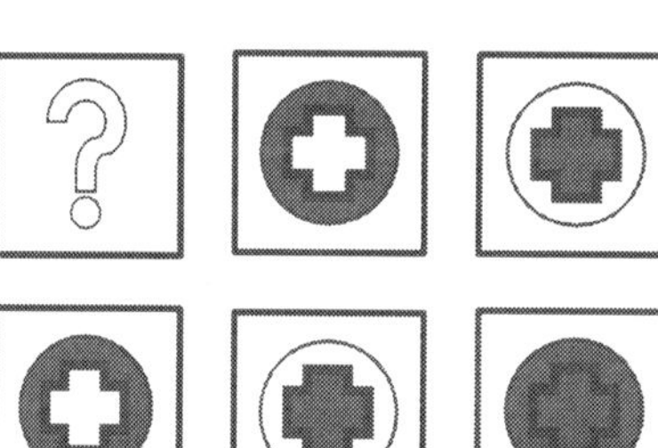

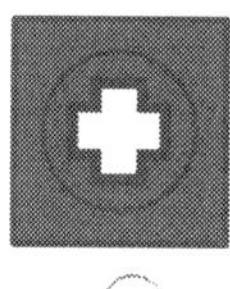

9.

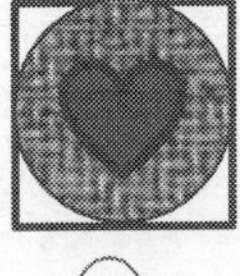
a

b

c

d

e

10.

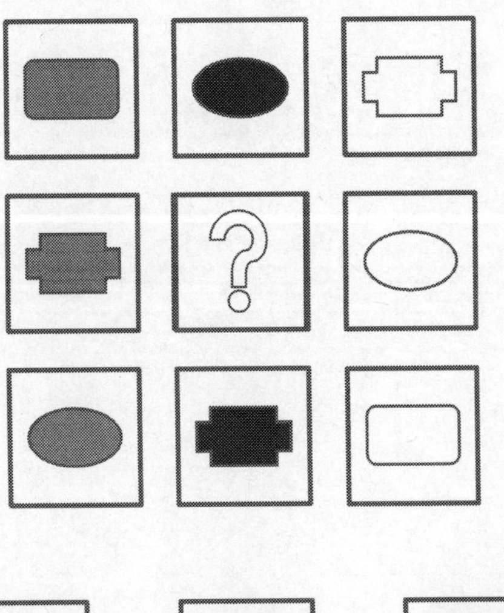

a b c d e

11.

a b c d e

SPATIAL VISUALIZATION – SECTION A

Each question in this section has three pictures on the top row. The third picture in the row is formed by combining the first two pictures. Using the same principle, pick the missing picture in the bottom row. Color the bubble under your choice.

1.

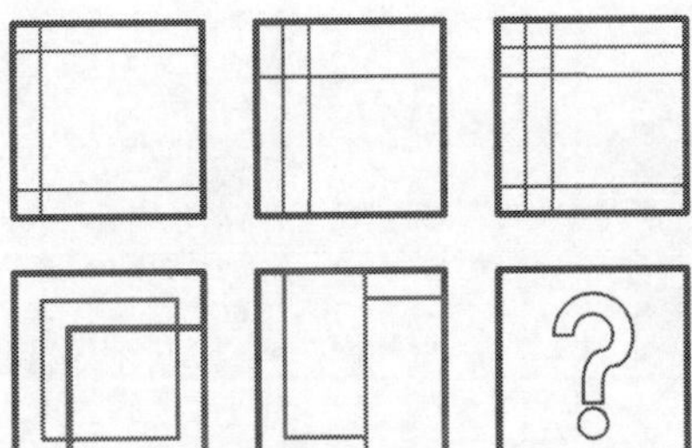

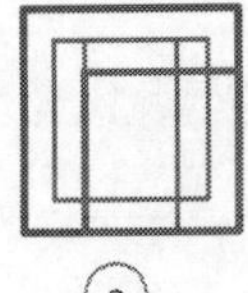
a

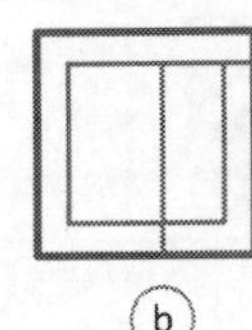
b

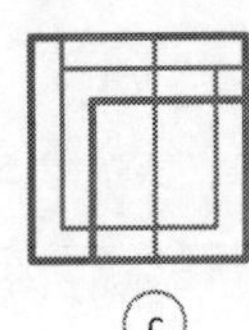
c

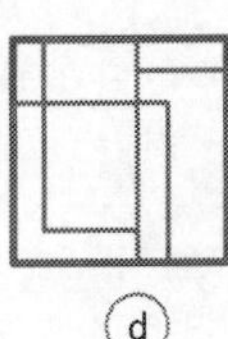
d

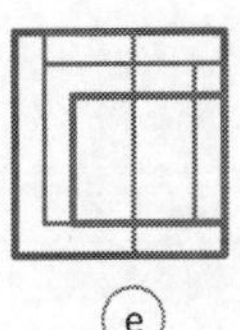
e

2.

a

b

c

d

e

3.

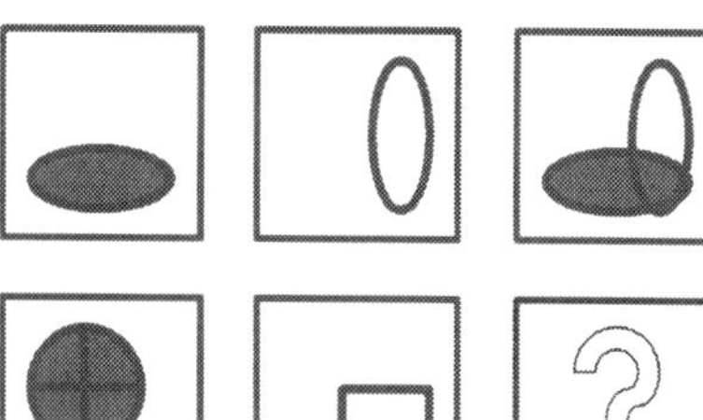

a

b

c

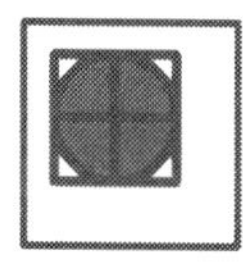
d

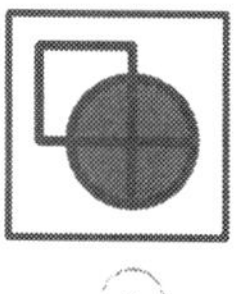
e

4.

a

b

c

d

e

5.

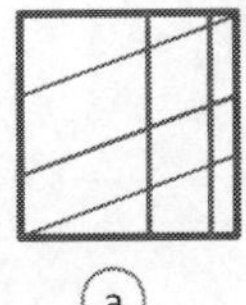
a

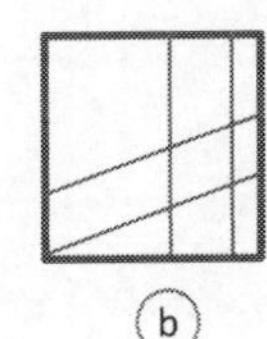
b

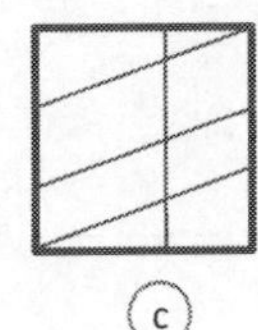
c

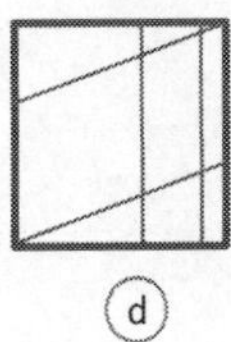
d

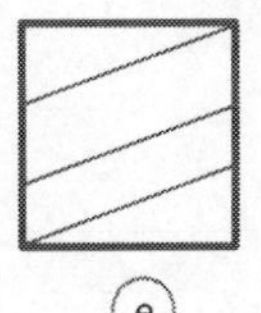
e

6.

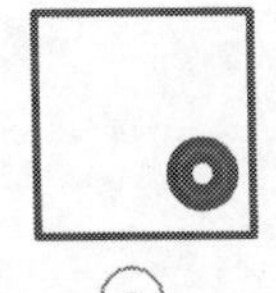
a

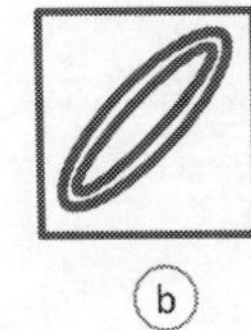
b

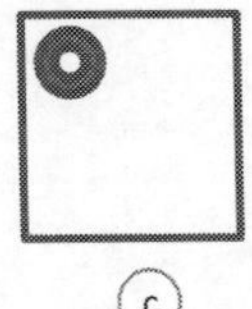
c

d

e

SPATIAL VISUALIZATION – SECTION B

Each question in this section has two pictures on the top row. The picture on the right in the top row is created by folding the outside shapes into the main shape of the picture on the left. Now, pick the picture that would be created when the outside shapes in the second row are folded in the same manner as the first row. Color the bubble under your choice.

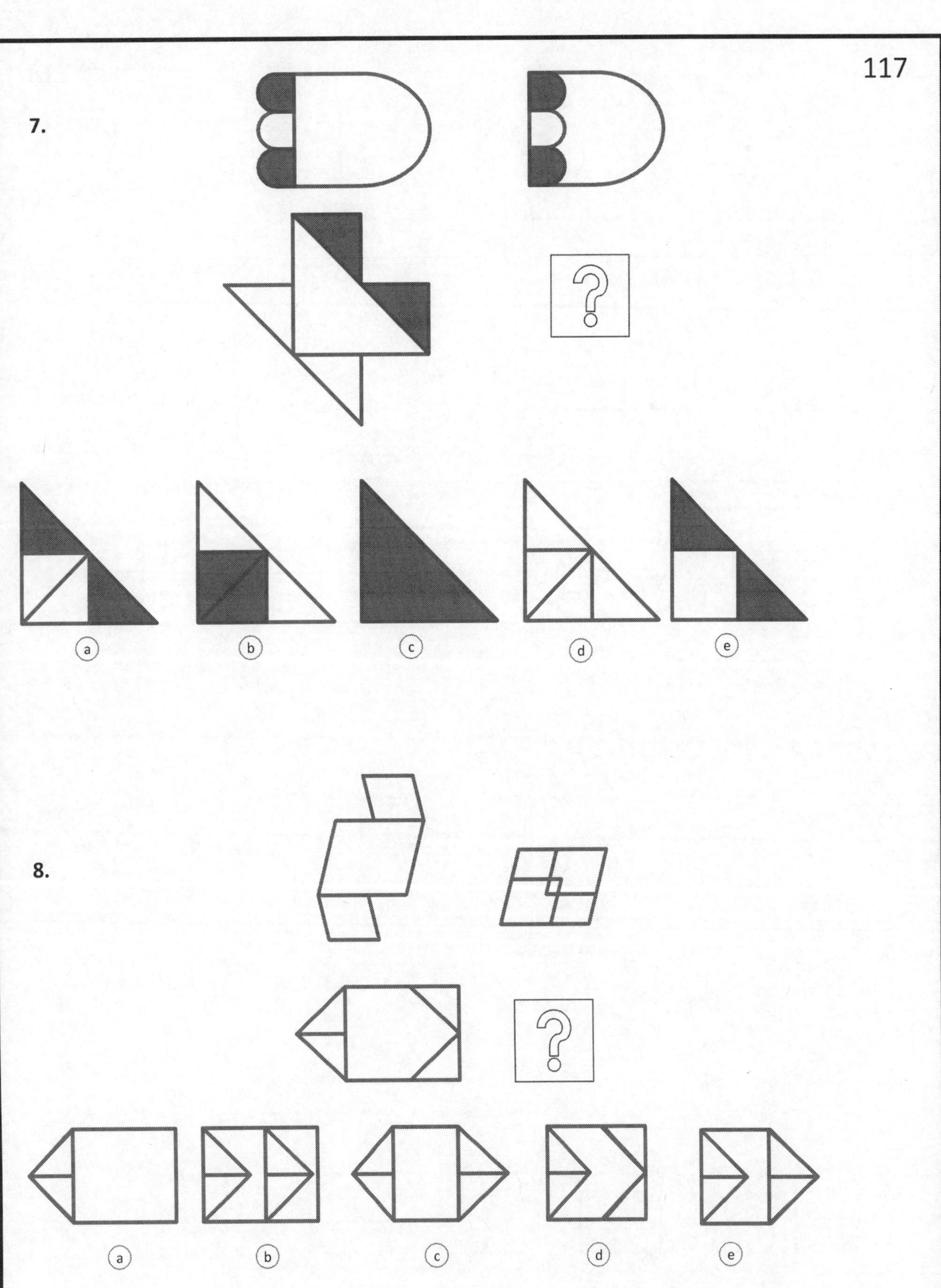
7.
a
b
c
d
e
8.
a
b
c
d
e

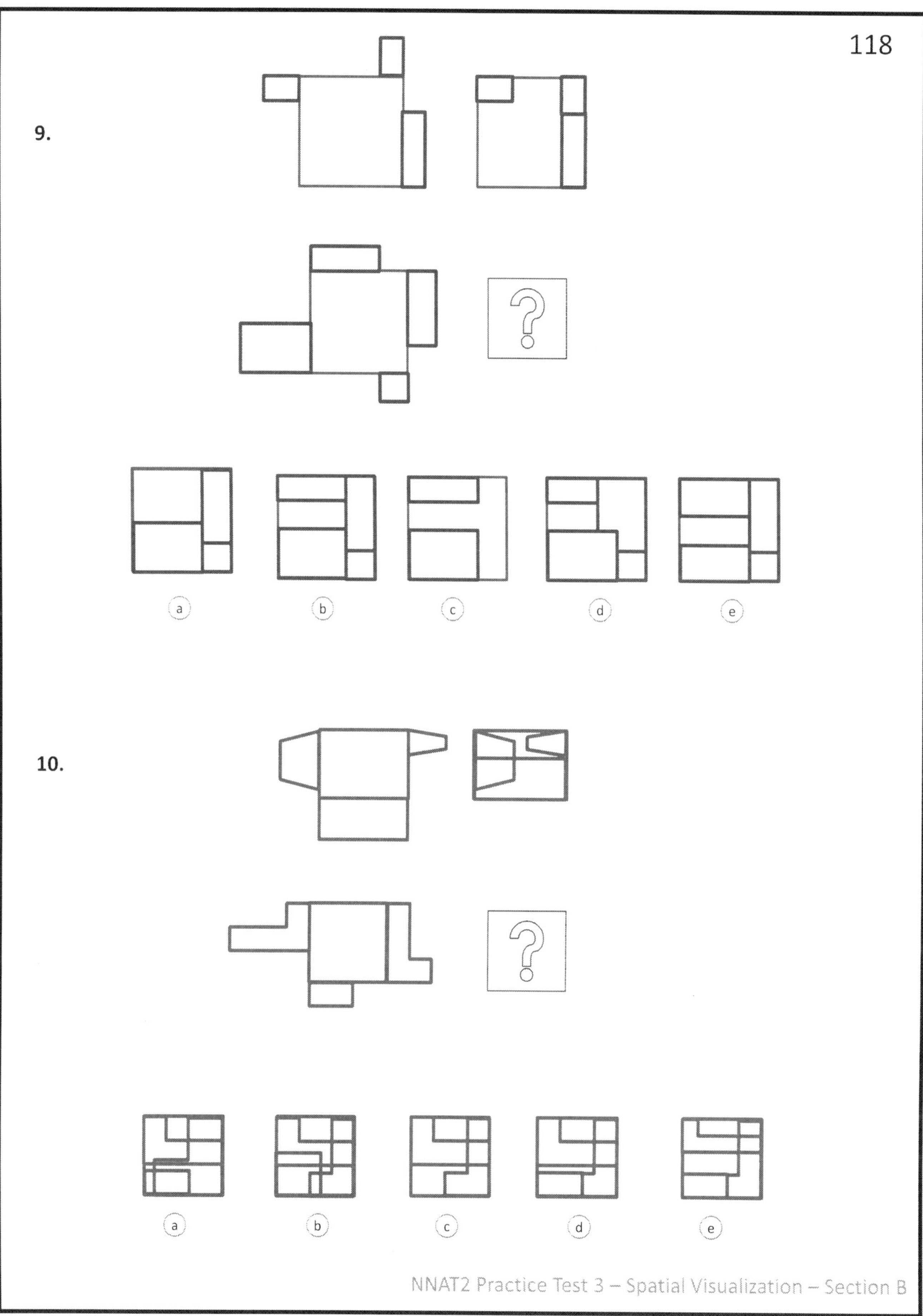
9.
a
b
c
d
e
10.
a
b
c
d
e

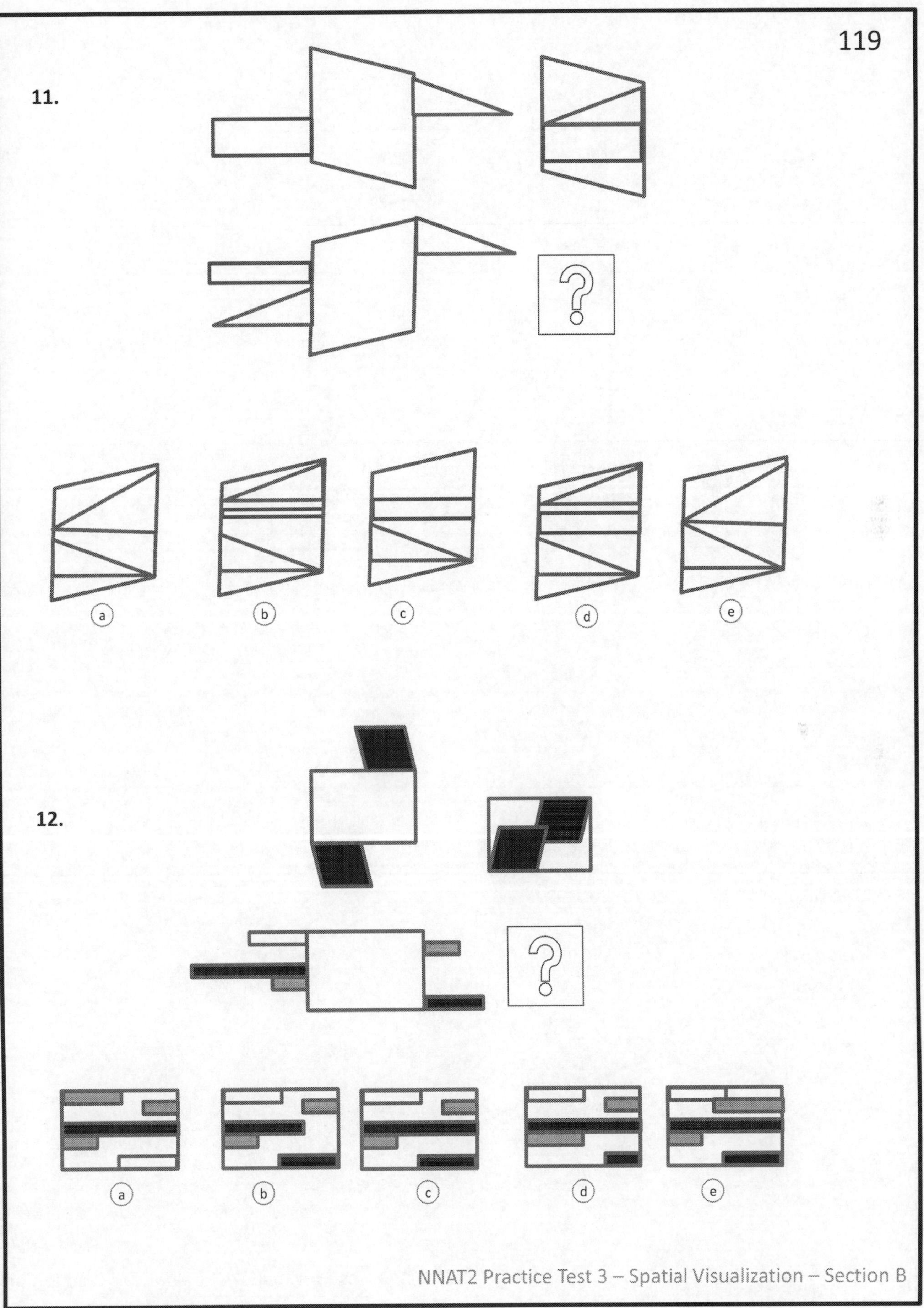
11.
a
b
c
d
e
12.
a
b
c
d
e

13.

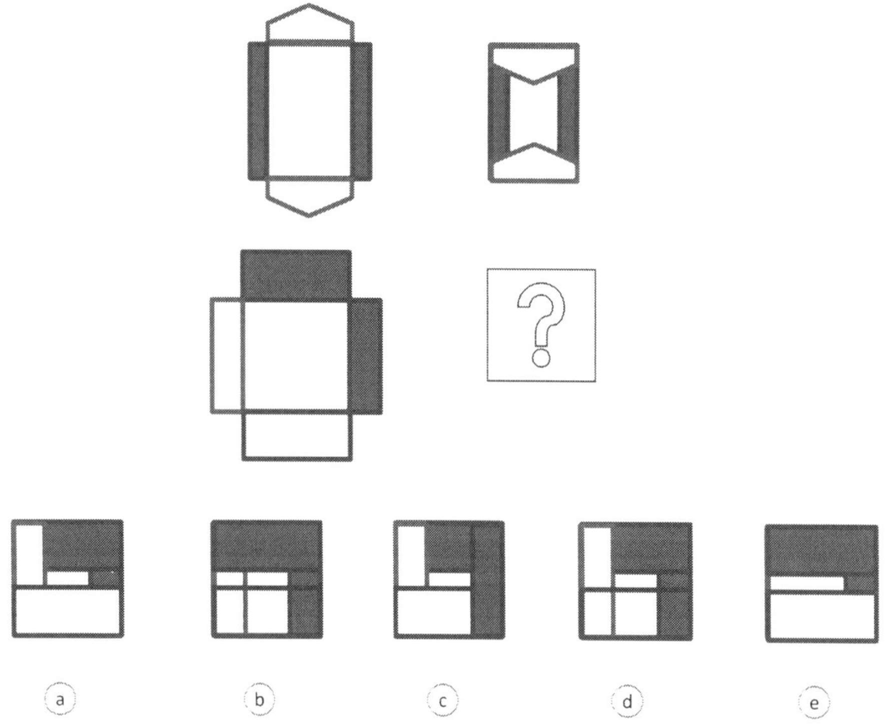

Practice Test 4 for the NNAT®2

Naglieri Nonverbal Ability Test®

Level D (Grades 3 & 4)

PATTERN COMPLETION

Each question in this section has a large rectangle with a picture or design. Within the large rectangle, there is a smaller rectangle with a question mark covering a section of the big rectangle. Pick the hidden part of the big rectangle and color the bubble under your choice.

1.

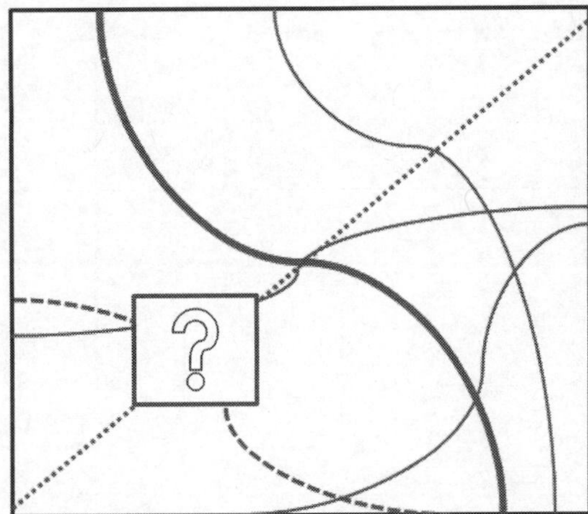

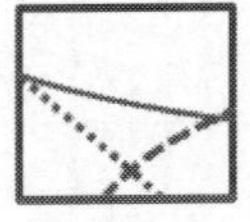
a

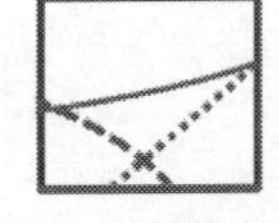
b

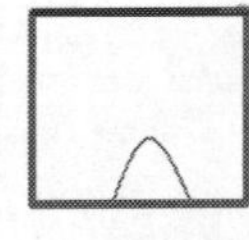
c

d

e

2.

a

b

c

d

e

3.

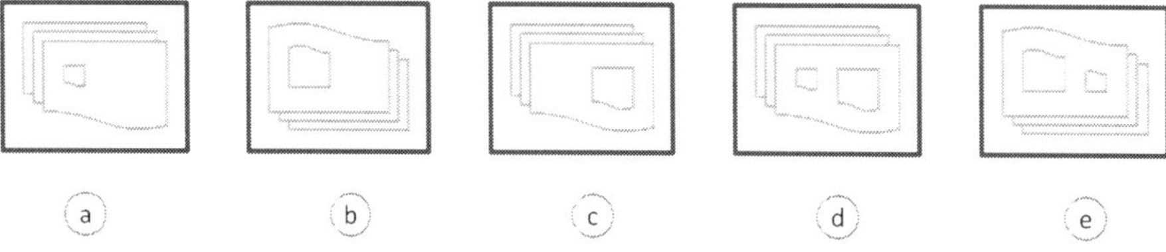

4.

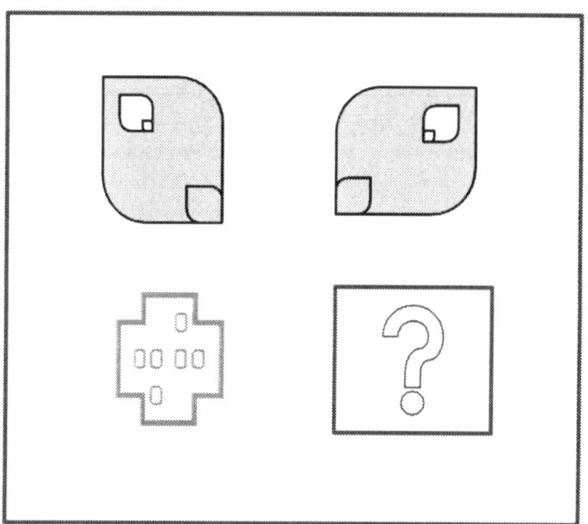

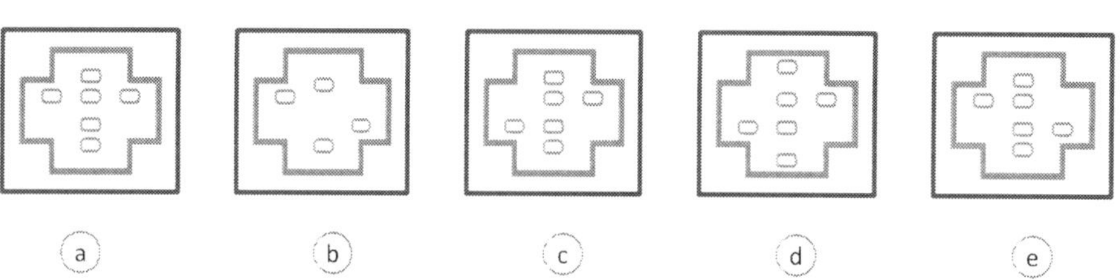

5.

a

b

c

d

e

6.

a

b

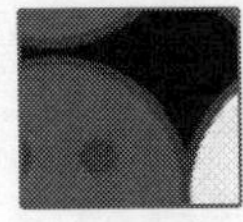
c

d

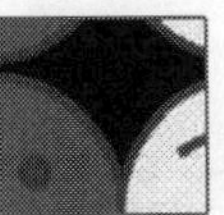
e

7.

a

b

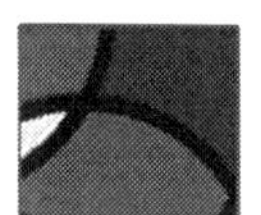
c

d

e

8.

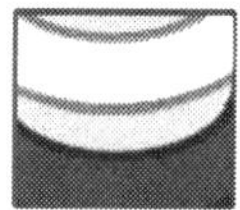
a

b

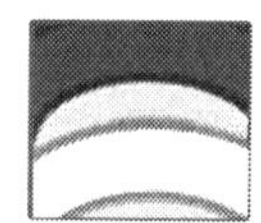
c

d

e

9.

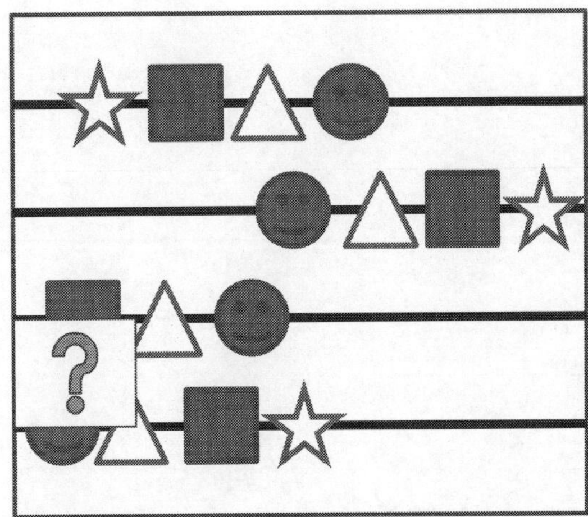

a

b

c

d

e

10.

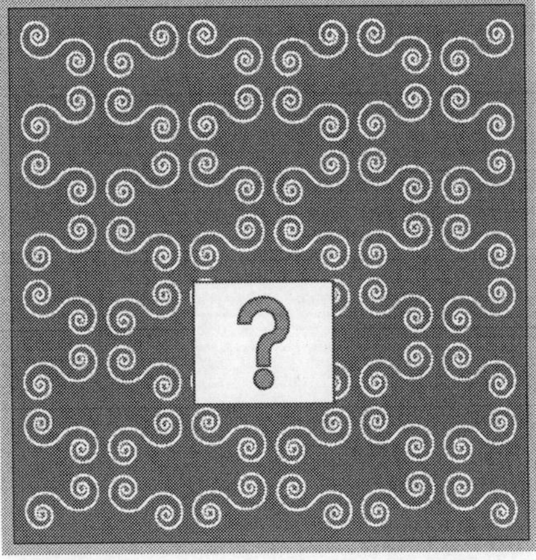

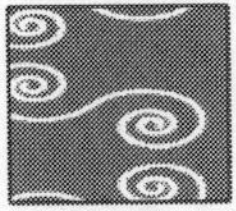

e

REASONING BY ANALOGY

Each question in this section has three rows of pictures. In each row, determine how the picture changes as you go across the row. The same changes should be echoed across all the three rows. Pick the missing picture and color the bubble under your choice.

1.

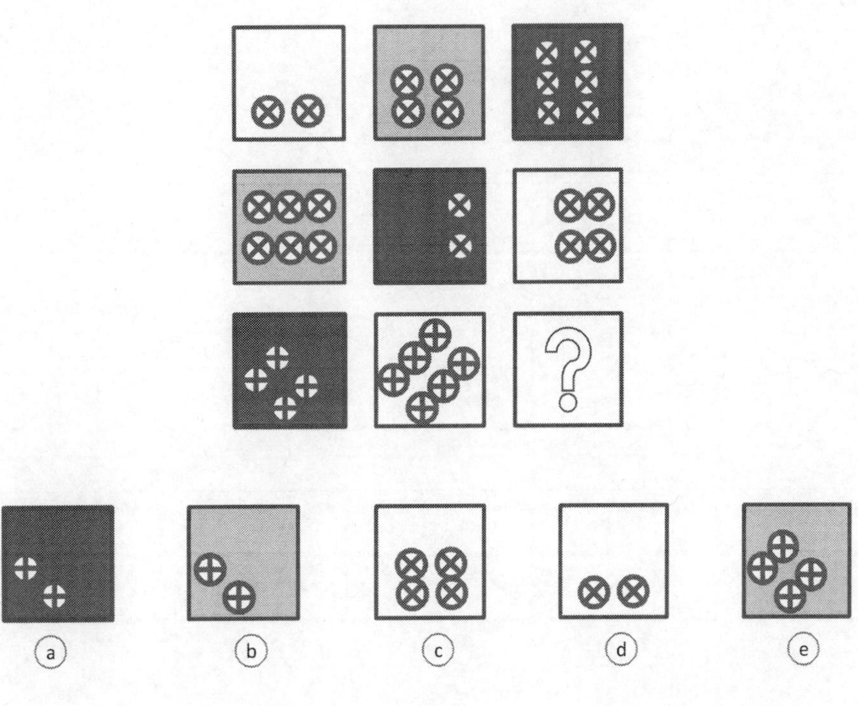

2.

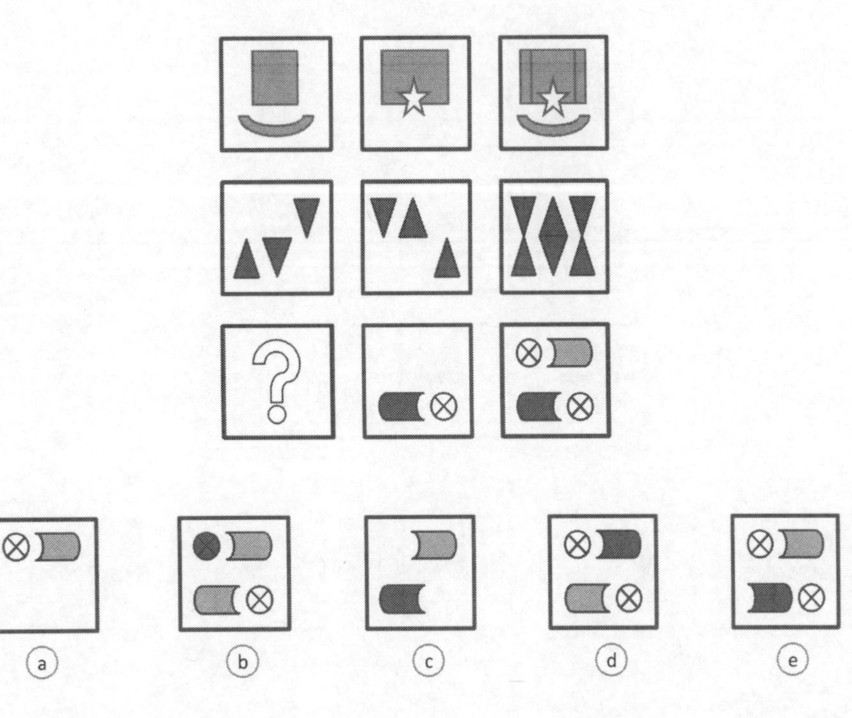

3.

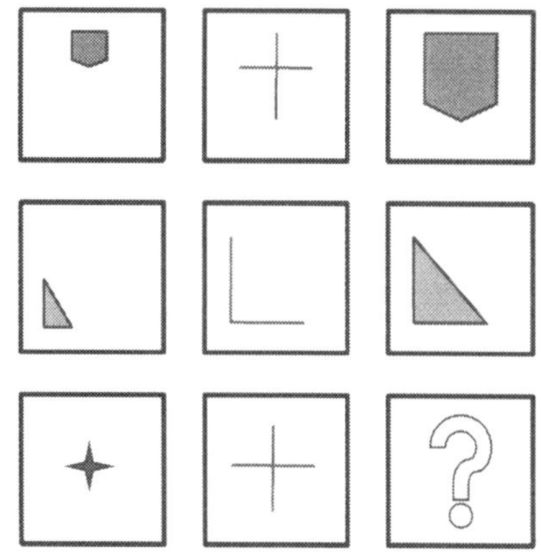

a

b

c

d

e

4.

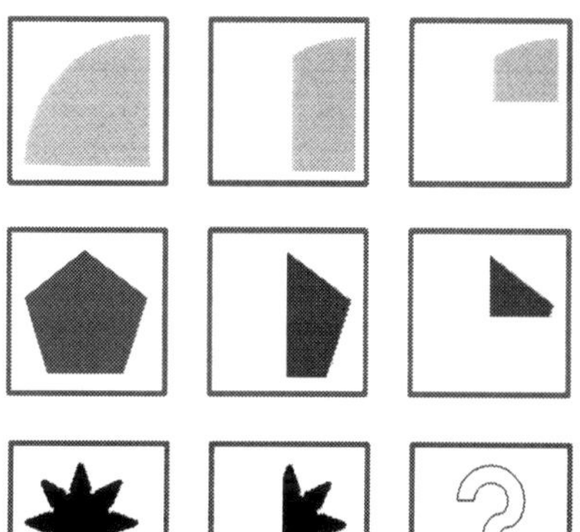

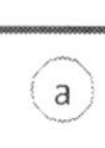

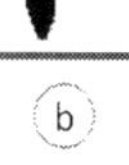

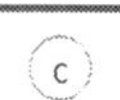

e

5.

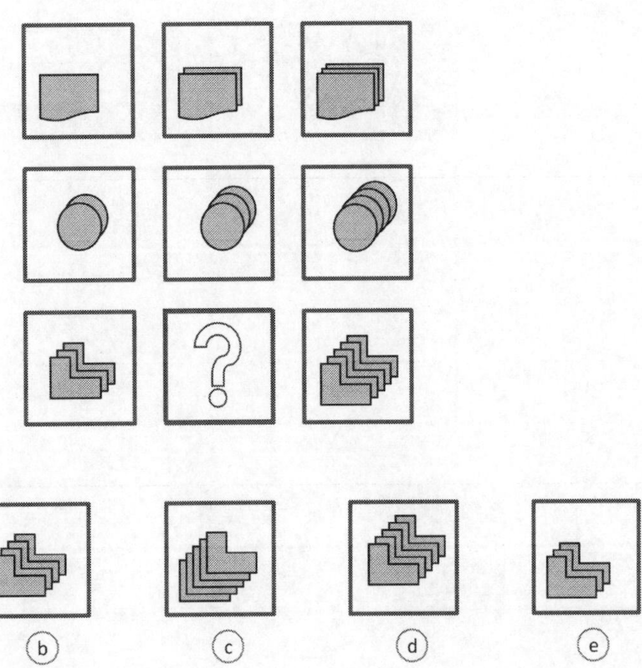

6.

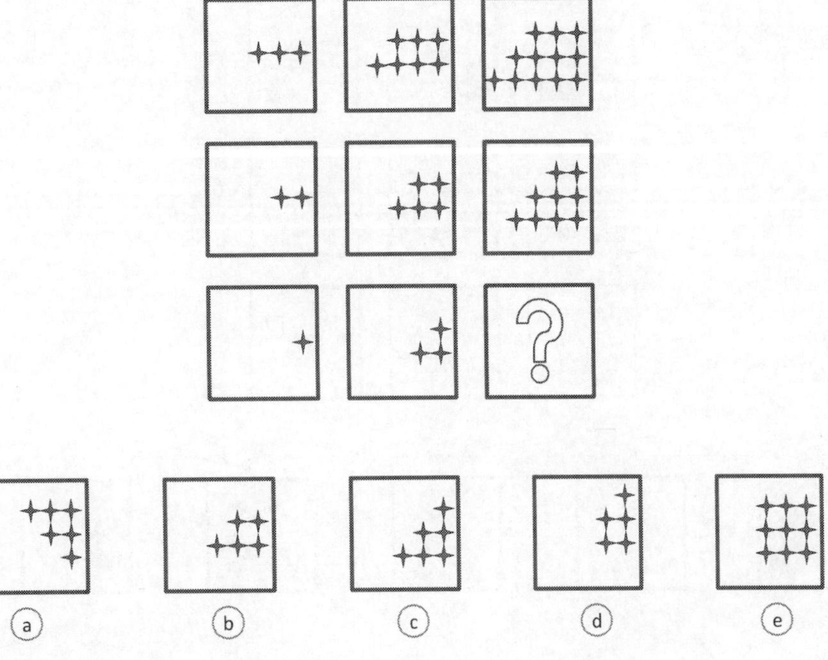

7.

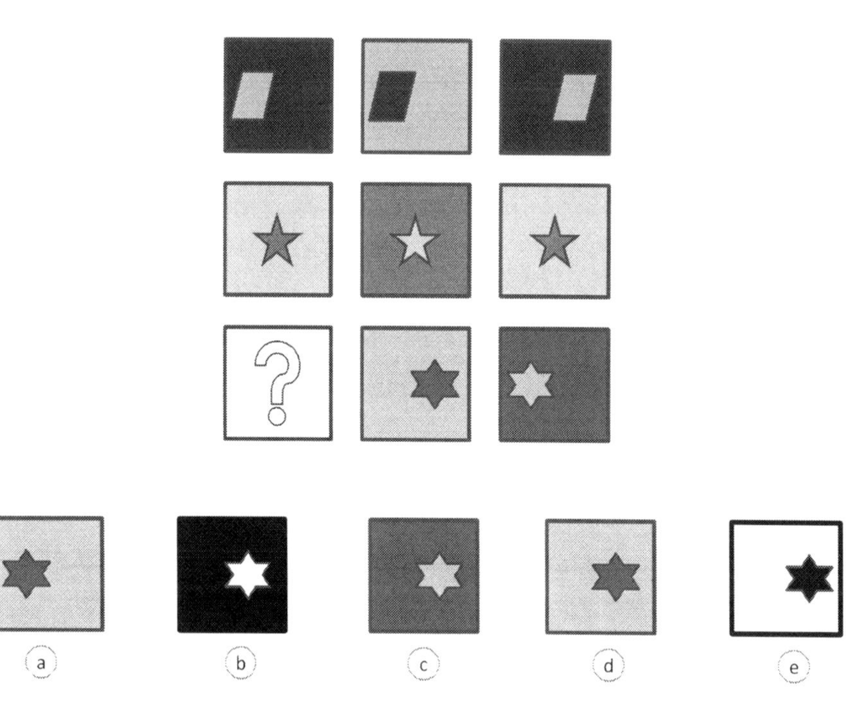

8.

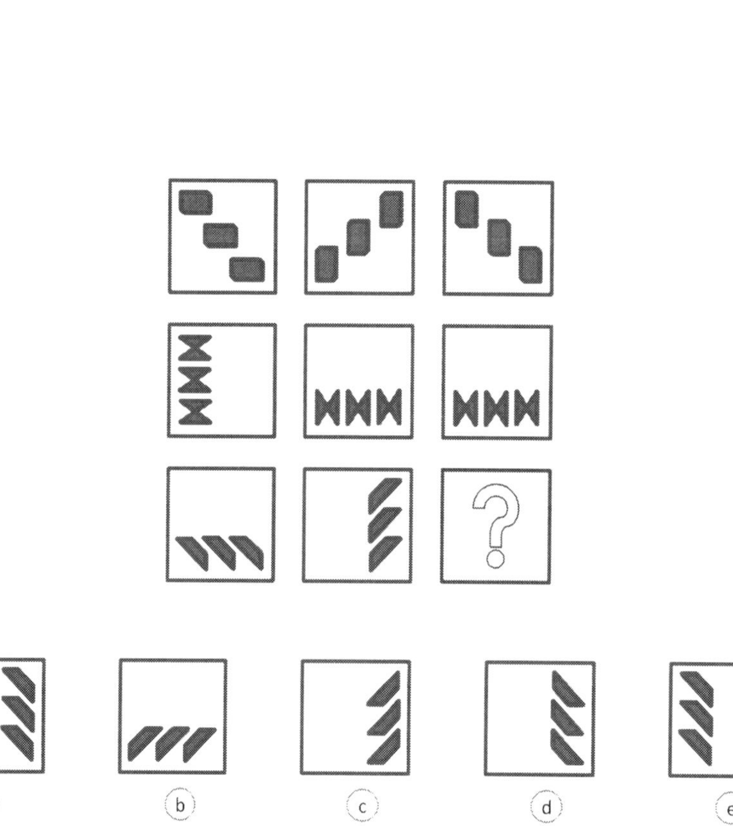

9.

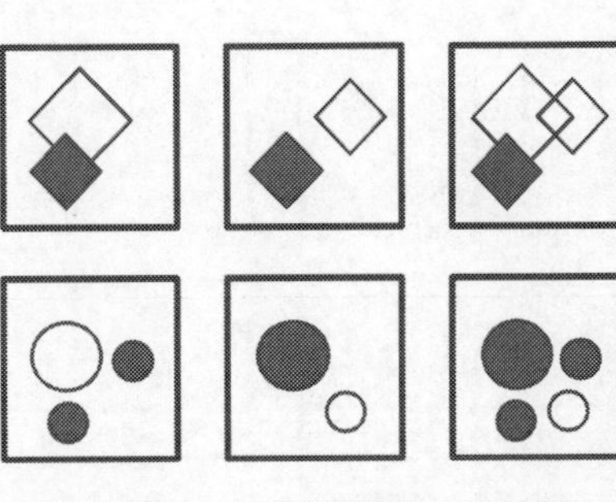

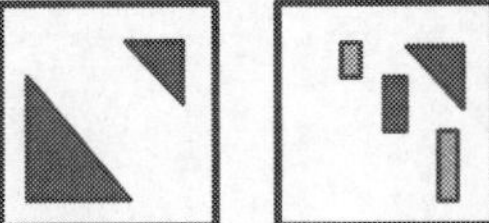

a b c d e

10.

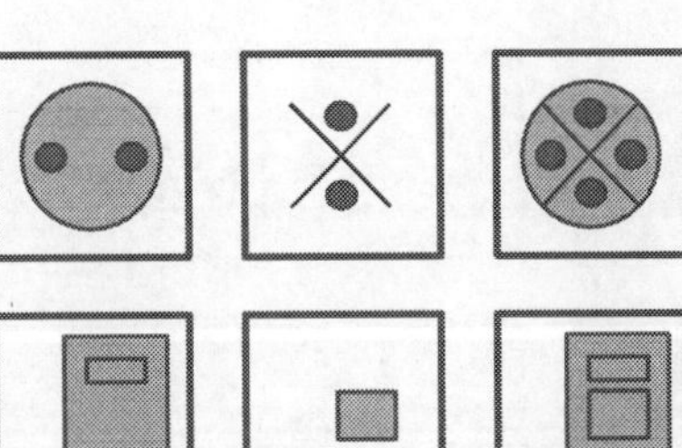

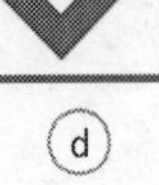

a b c d e

11.

a

b

c

d

e

12.

a

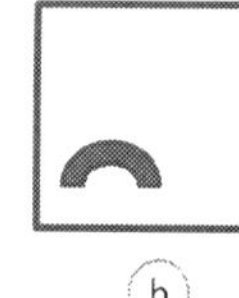
b

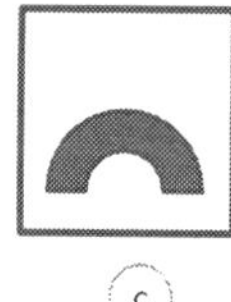
c

d

e

13.

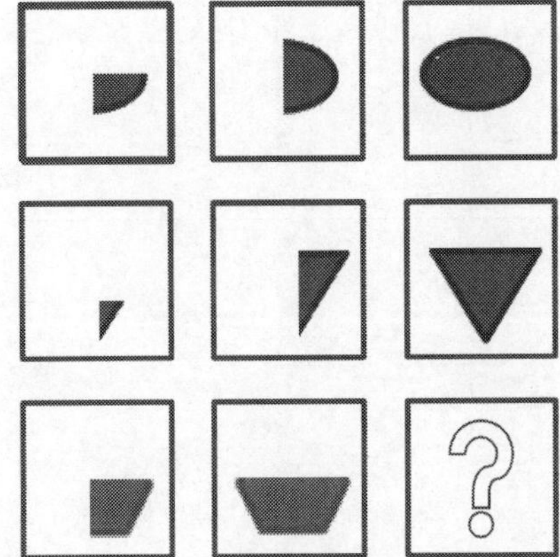

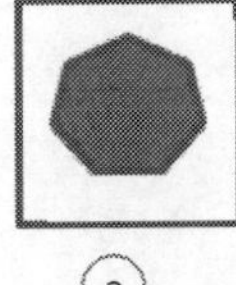
a

b

c

d

e

14.

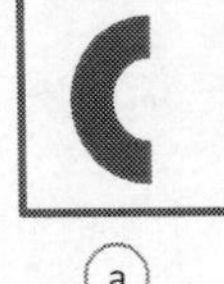
a

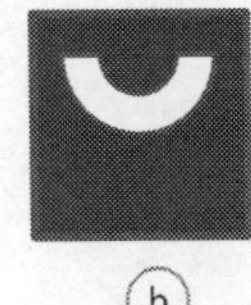
b

c

d

e

SERIAL REASONING

Each question in this section has a matrix of three rows and three columns. The pictures change as you go across the row and down the column in the matrix. Determine the change pattern within the matrix and pick the correct missing picture that will complete the matrix. Color the bubble under your choice.

1.

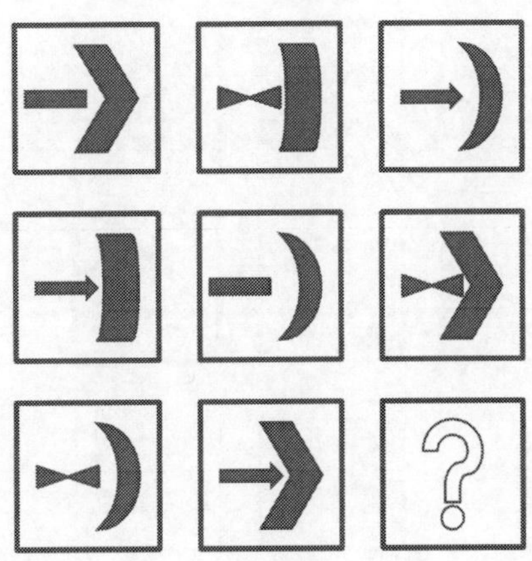

(a)

(b)

(c)

(d)

(e)

2.

(a)

(b)

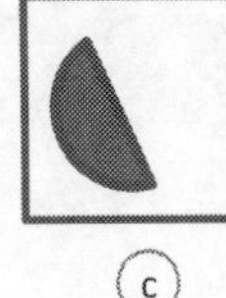

(c)

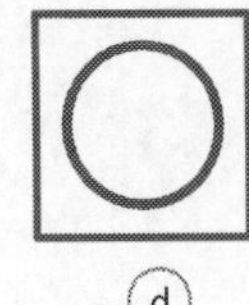

(d)

(e)

3.

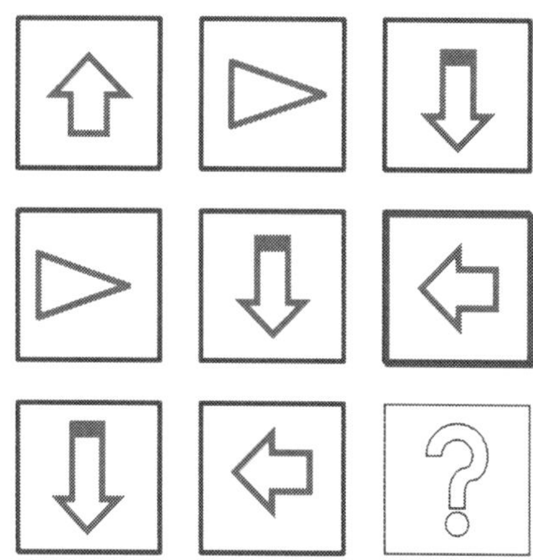

a

b

c

d

e

4.

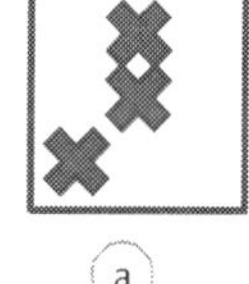
a

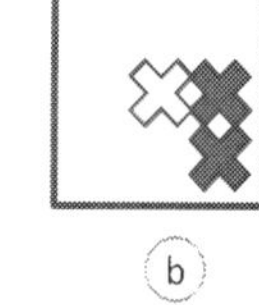
b

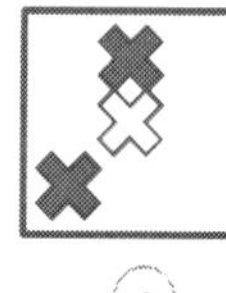
c

d

e

5.

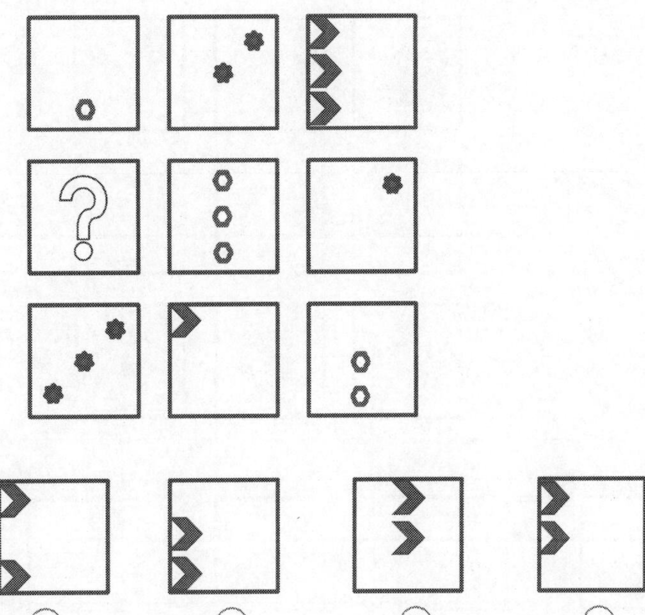

6.

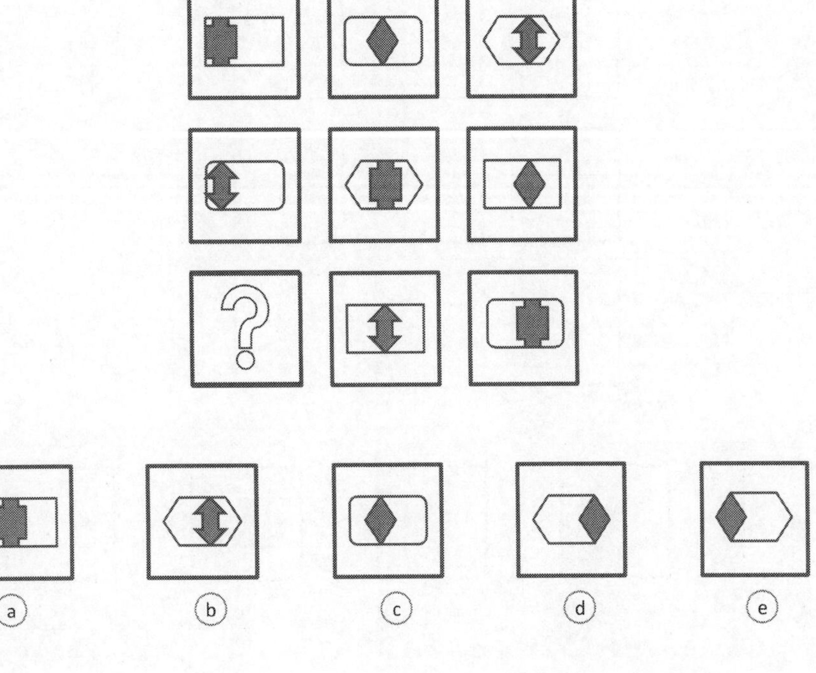

7.

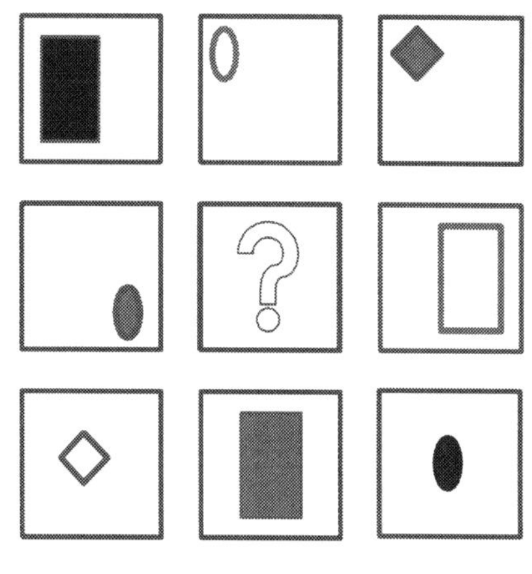

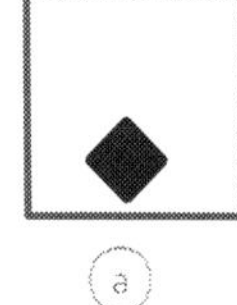
a

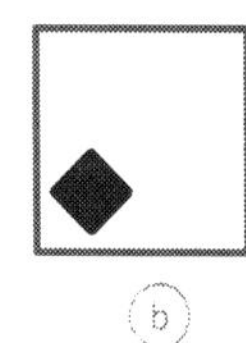
b

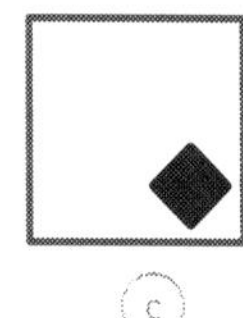
c

d

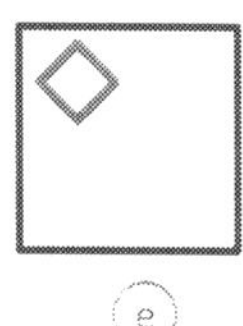
e

8.

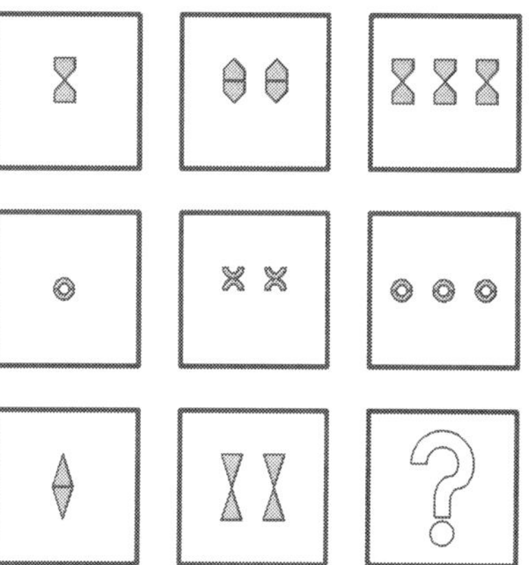

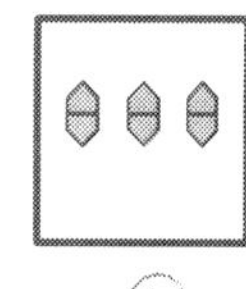

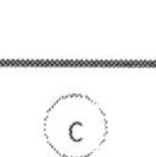

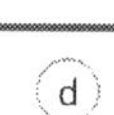

e

9.

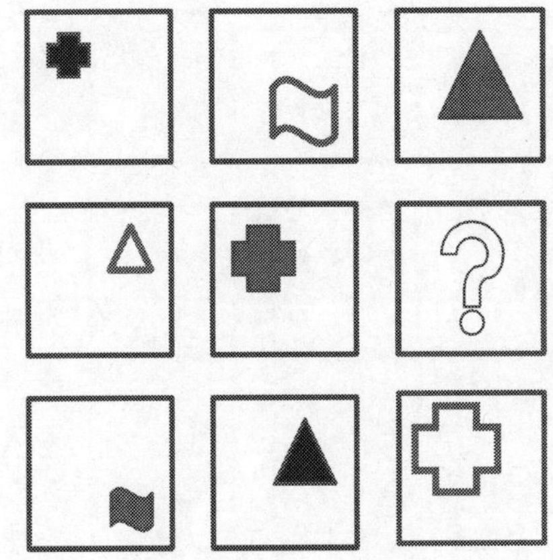

a

b

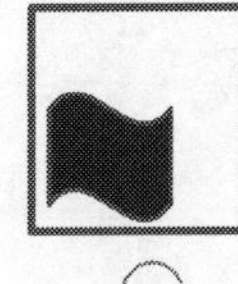
c

d

e

10.

a b c d e

11.

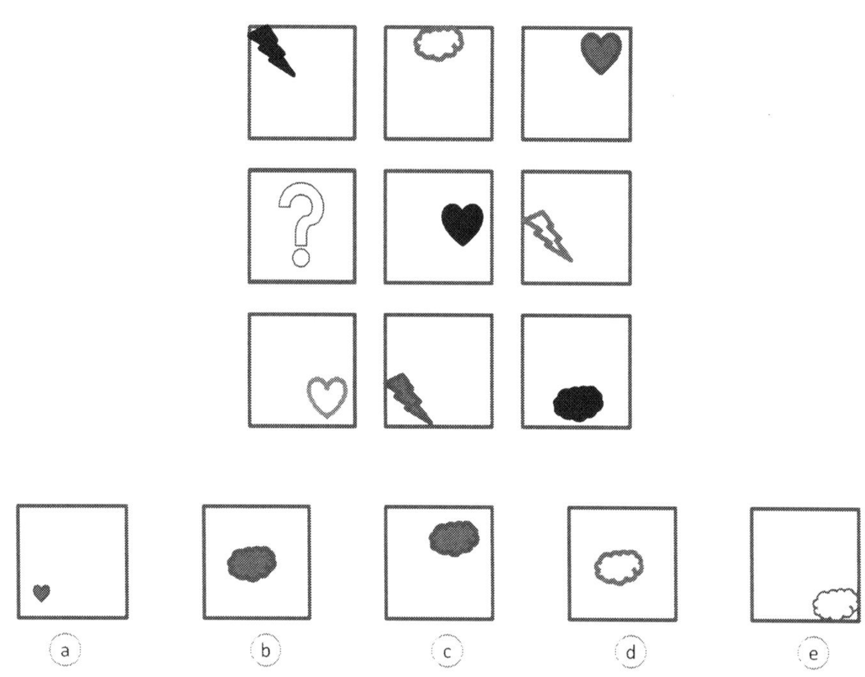

SPATIAL VISUALIZATION – SECTION A

Each question in this section has three pictures on the top row. The third picture in the row is formed by combining the first two pictures. Using the same principle, pick the missing picture in the bottom row. Color the bubble under your choice.

1.

a

b

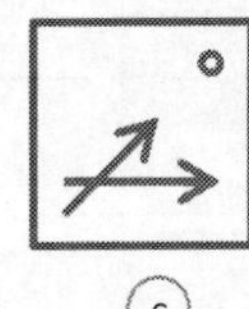

c

d

e

2.

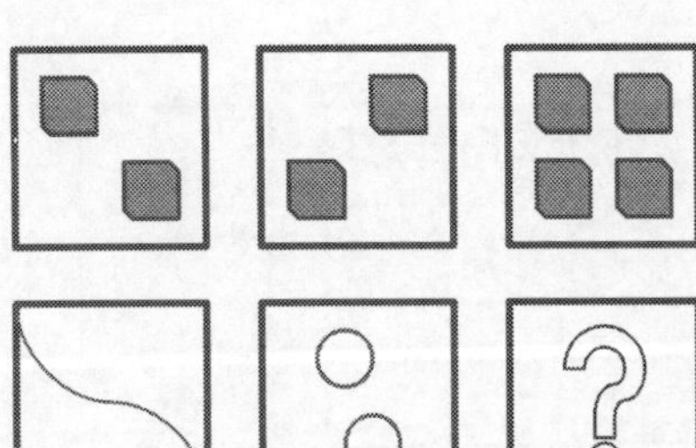

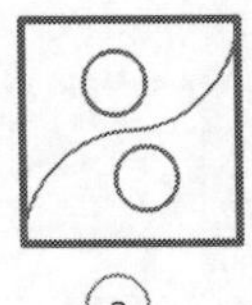

a

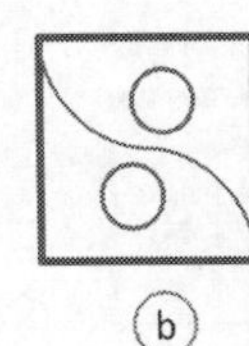

b

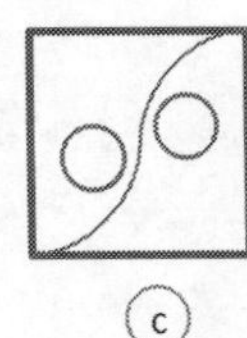

c

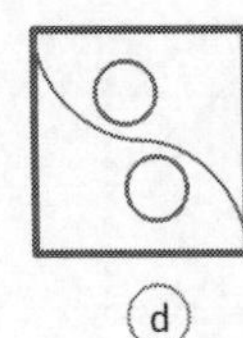

d

e

3.

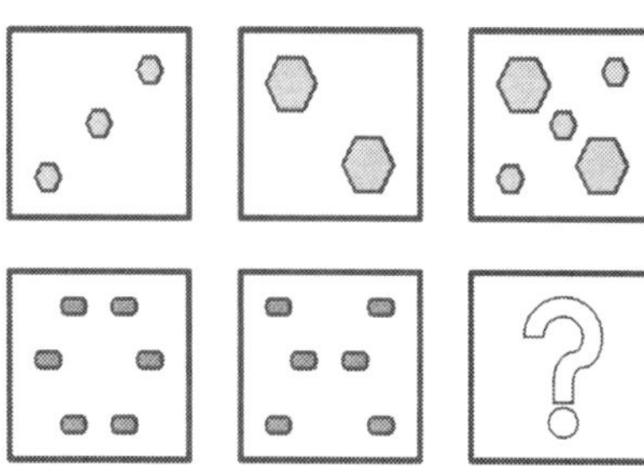

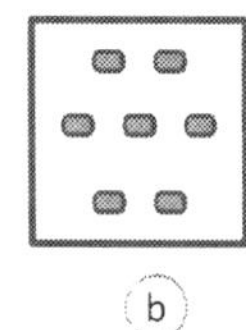
a

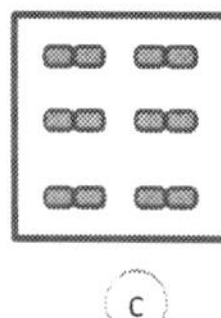
b

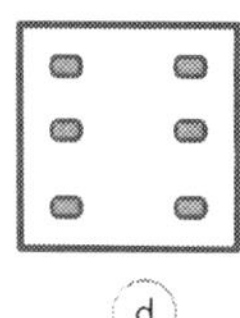
c

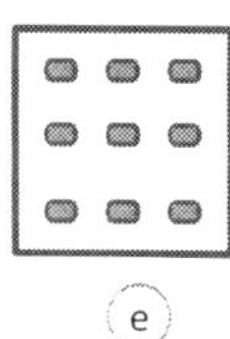
d

e

4.

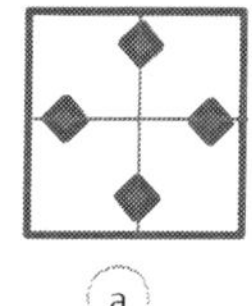
a

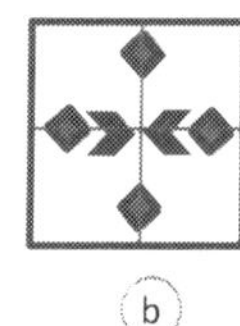
b

c

d

e

5.

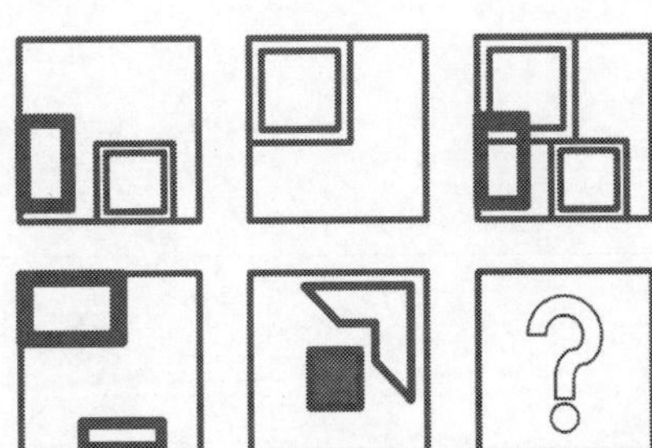

a

b

c

d

e

6.

a

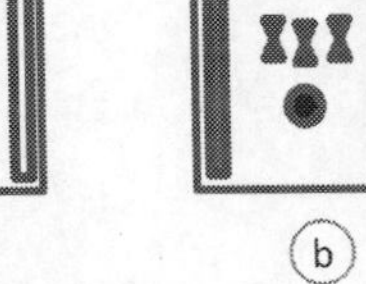
b

c

d

e

SPATIAL VISUALIZATION – SECTION B

Each question in this section has two pictures on the top row. The picture on the right in the top row is created by folding the outside shapes into the main shape of the picture on the left. Now, pick the picture that would be created when the outside shapes in the second row are folded in the same manner as the first row. Color the bubble under your choice.

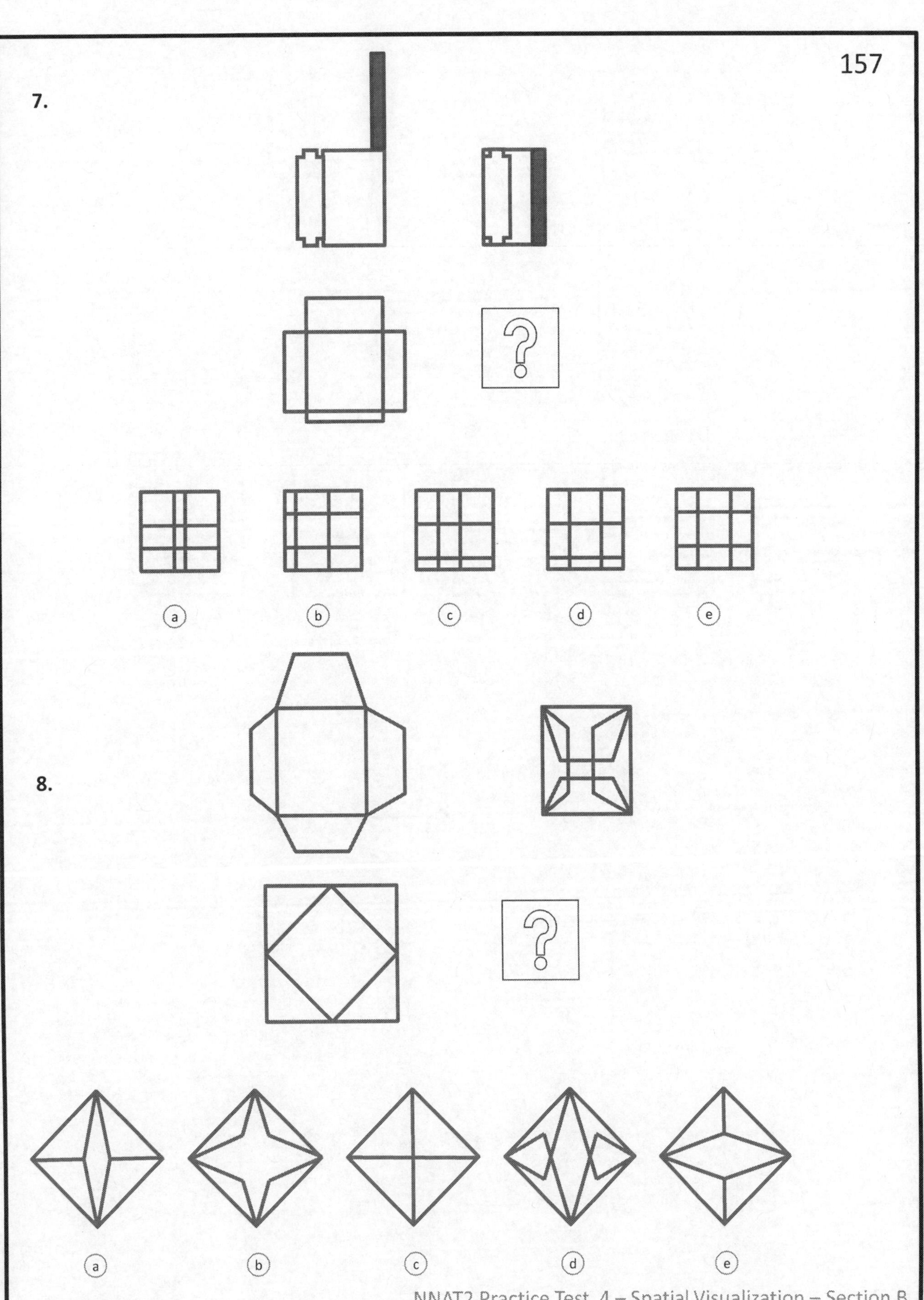
7.
a
b
c
d
e
8.
a
b
c
d
e

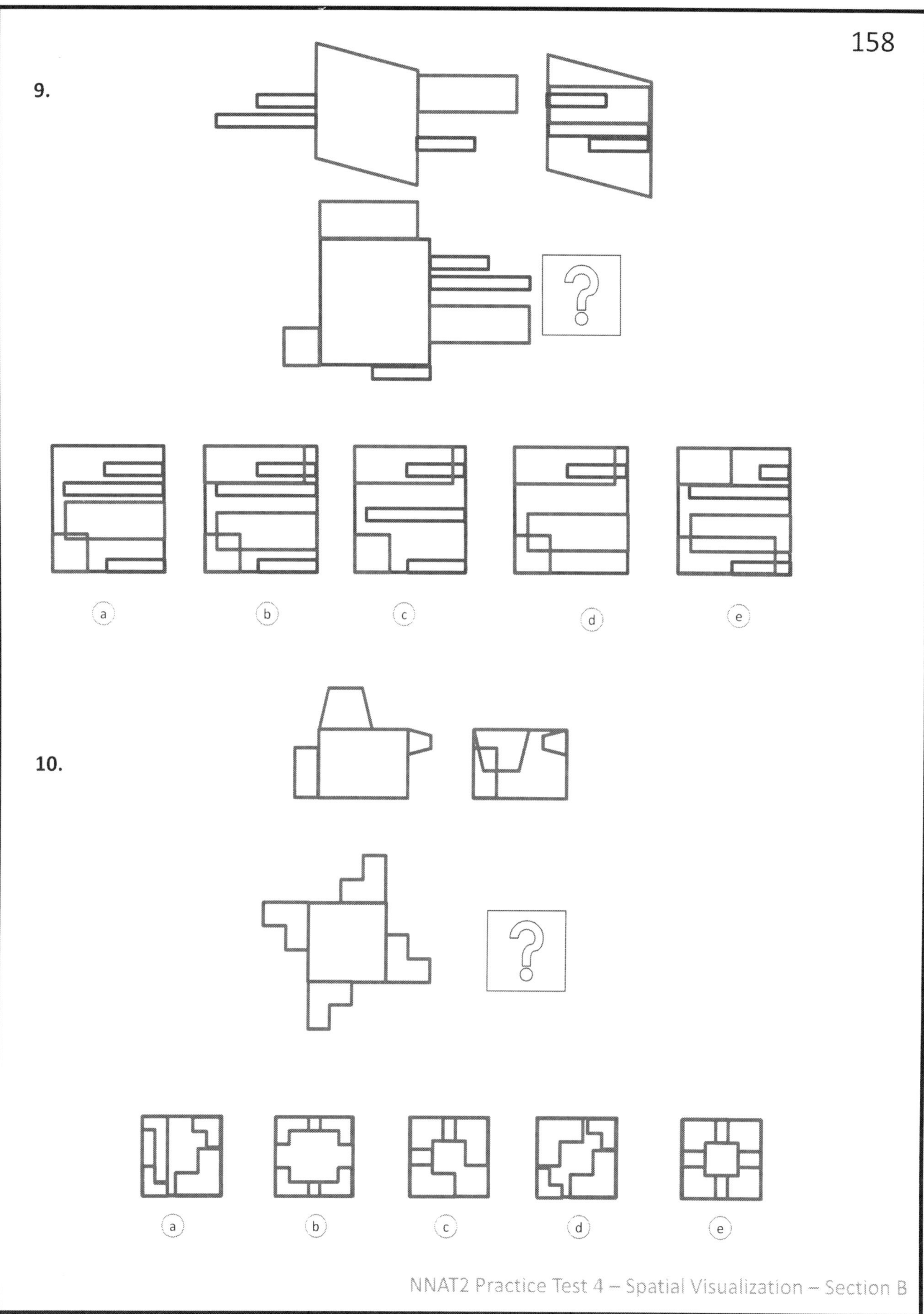
9.
a
b
c
d
e
10.
a
b
c
d
e

11.

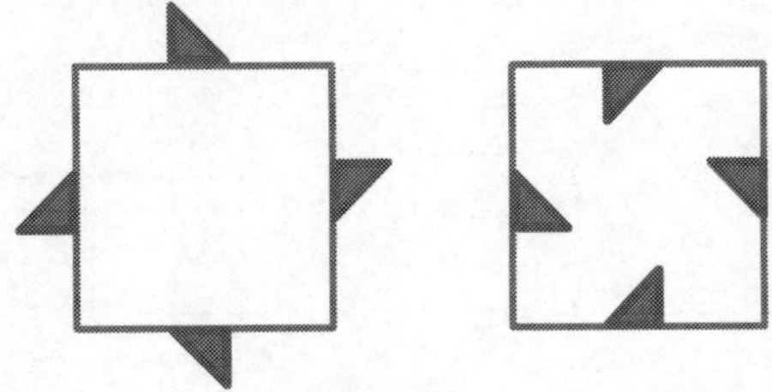

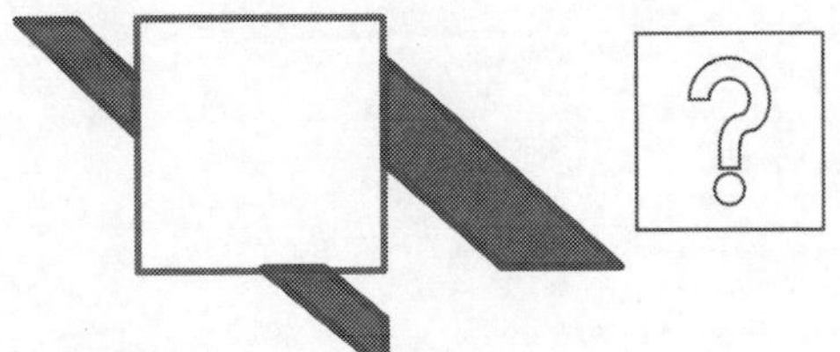

a

b

c

d

e

12.

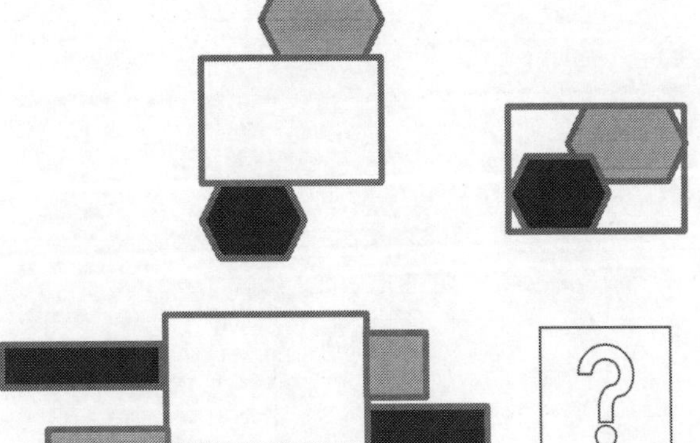

a

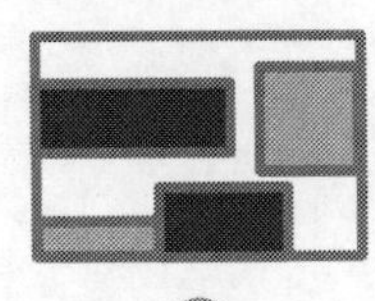
b

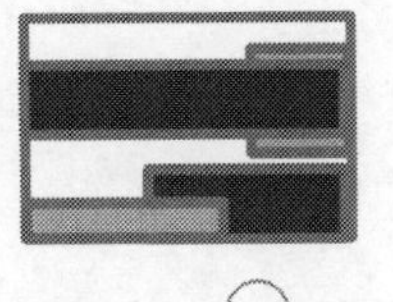
c

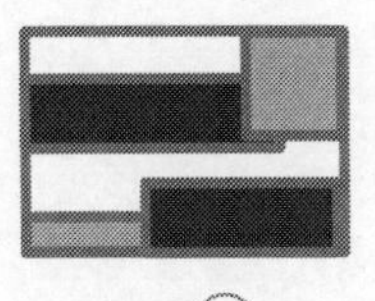
d

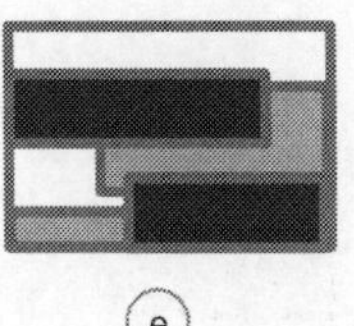
e

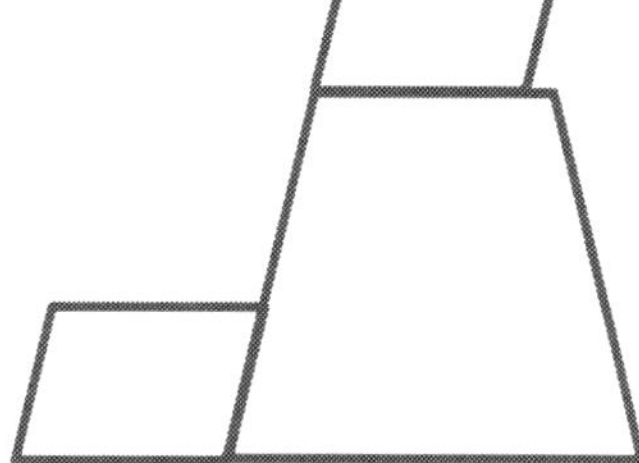

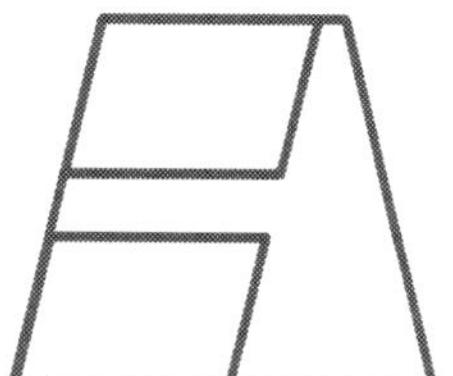

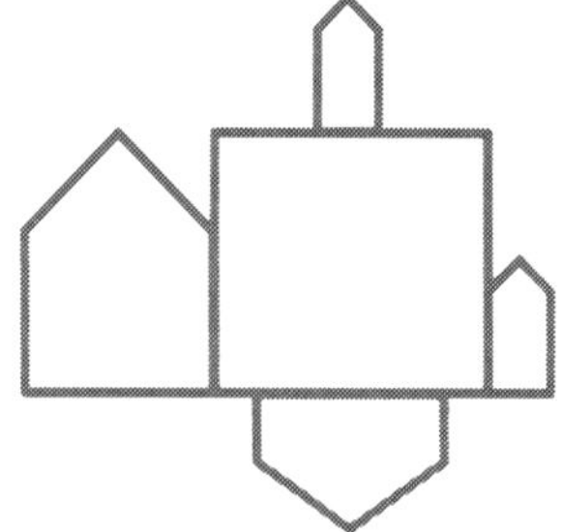

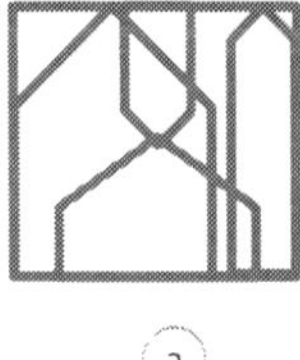

a b c d e

ANSWER KEY

NNAT®2 PRACTICE TEST 1 – ANSWER KEY

Pattern Completion – 10 questions

1. c
2. e
3. e
4. c
5. d
6. a
7. d
8. a
9. a
10. a

Reasoning by Analogy– 14 questions

1. d
2. a
3. d
4. a
5. a
6. c
7. e
8. a
9. e
10. c
11. d
12. c
13. a
14. c

NNAT®2 PRACTICE TEST 1 – ANSWER KEY

Serial Reasoning – 11 questions

1. b
2. c
3. a
4. a
5. b
6. d
7. b
8. e
9. b
10. e
11. d

Spatial Visualization – 13 questions

1. d
2. a
3. b
4. c
5. a
6. b
7. c
8. c
9. a
10. b
11. c
12. b
13. c

NNAT®2 PRACTICE TEST 2 – ANSWER KEY

Pattern Completion – 10 questions

1. c
2. a
3. e
4. a
5. d
6. b
7. b
8. d
9. d
10. a

Reasoning by Analogy– 14 questions

1. b
2. c
3. d
4. e
5. c
6. c
7. d
8. e
9. a
10. e
11. d
12. e
13. a
14. b

NNAT®2 PRACTICE TEST 2 – ANSWER KEY

Serial Reasoning – 11 questions

1. c
2. e
3. d
4. c
5. c
6. a
7. a
8. b
9. c
10. a
11. d

Spatial Visualization – 13 questions

1. a
2. d
3. c
4. b
5. e
6. a
7. c
8. b
9. a
10. d
11. c
12. e
13. e

NNAT®2 PRACTICE TEST 3 – ANSWER KEY

Pattern Completion – 10 questions

1. d
2. a
3. c
4. e
5. b
6. d
7. b
8. c
9. e
10. e

Reasoning by Analogy– 14 questions

1. c
2. e
3. a
4. a
5. c
6. d
7. a
8. b
9. a
10. d
11. b
12. c
13. c
14. e

NNAT®2 PRACTICE TEST 3 – ANSWER KEY

Serial Reasoning – 11 questions

1. d
2. b
3. e
4. d
5. b
6. a
7. d
8. a
9. c
10. d
11. d

Spatial Visualization – 13 questions

1. c
2. d
3. b
4. e
5. a
6. c
7. a
8. e
9. b
10. d
11. d
12. c
13. a

NNAT®2 PRACTICE TEST 4 – ANSWER KEY

Pattern Completion – 10 questions

1. d
2. a
3. c
4. e
5. a
6. e
7. a
8. b
9. e
10. d

Reasoning by Analogy– 14 questions

1. b
2. a
3. a
4. c
5. b
6. c
7. c
8. e
9. c
10. e
11. a
12. a
13. b
14. d

NNAT®2 PRACTICE TEST 4 – ANSWER KEY

Serial Reasoning – 11 questions

1. d
2. e
3. b
4. c
5. e
6. e
7. c
8. a
9. d
10. e
11. b

Spatial Visualization – 13 questions

1. a
2. d
3. c
4. b
5. c
6. e
7. d
8. c
9. b
10. e
11. c
12. a
13. d

47997012R00101

Made in the USA
Middletown, DE
08 September 2017